22260 -2

LC
3731
B66

Brembeck, Cole
Speicher.

Cultural challenges
to education

DATE		
DEC 5 '74		
MAY 5 '91		
FEB 11 '92		
NOV 07 '95		
MAY - 6 1997		
JUL - 9 1998		
JUL 06 2004		
JUN 12 2008		
NOV 06 2016		

© THE BAKER & TAYLOR CO.

**Cultural Challenges
to Education**

Cultural Challenges to Education

The Influence of Cultural Factors in School Learning

Cole S. Brembeck
Michigan State University

Walker H. Hill
Michigan State University
Editors

Lexington Books
D.C. Heath and Company
Lexington, Massachusetts
Toronto   London

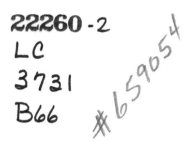
Library of Congress Cataloging in Publication Data

Brembeck, Cole Speicher.
   Cultural challenges to education.

     1. Minorities—Education—United States—Addresses,
essays, lectures.   2. Intercultural education—
Addresses, essays, lectures.   3. Educational anthro-
pology—Addresses, essays, lectures.   I. Hill, Walker
H., joint author.   II. Title.
LC3731.B66   370.19'34   73-9734
ISBN 0-669-90324-8

Contents

Preface

Individual differences were once thought to be the only important ones in a child's learning; cultural differences didn't count for much. Now we are beginning to see that, when children succeed or fail in school, they do so not just as individuals but as members of groups having common social characteristics. The matter exceeds the question of why Mary succeeds while Angela fails; it becomes one of cultural characteristics and differences. The larger environment in which individuals live thus becomes the arena for exploring the influence and uses of cultural values in school learning and educational decision making.

The aim of this book is to explore this arena in such a way that we are better able to: (1) identify cultural characteristics and differences, (2) appreciate and respect them, and (3) learn to use them constructively in educational planning and school learning.

This threefold purpose is somewhat at variance with common practice. Observation suggests that a great many teachers and planners find it difficult to identify cultural differences, tend to downgrade them when they are identified, and see few possibilities for their positive use in stimulating a child's learning. In spite of past trends we believe the tide is turning in favor of a new recognition of the role of cultural values in school learning and how they may be employed to bring a new synthesis to education and culture. It is hoped that this book will lend encouragement to the trend.

Many of the ideas presented here and their inception in a seminar convened by the senior editor of this volume under the auspices of the East-West Center in Honolulu. The participants were internationally known scholars who were invited to examine the role of the schools in a period of rapid social and cultural change. Seminar participants brought drafts of ideas with them for the group to discuss and debate. After the seminar some participants expressed an interest in continuing the work in order to test and further develop the ideas generated in the sharp exchange of the meeting. Out of this process some papers came to publishable form and we are pleased to present them in this volume. Other papers included here were either prepared, upon invitation, or selected from other sources.

What are the uses of this book? We hope that the widening interest in the educational uses of cultural characteristics will invite a large general readership. More specifically, we have selected and developed papers with a view to their usefulness for both prospective and experienced teachers and for other educational decision makers. Interest in the influence of culture on education seems to be growing rapidly among professional educators. It is heartening to see the establishment of new departments in education devoted to social and cultural concerns and new courses to focus this concern. Existing courses also are being revised to include the cultural dimension. We believe *Cultural Challenges to Education* will serve as a useful text in courses like these and help to stimulate exciting classroom discussion in a subject that is as current as today's headlines.

We wish to express our appreciation to the East-West Center for turning our heads in the direction of a subject of gathering importance. We thank the Southwestern Cooperative Educational Laboratory, Albuquerque, New Mexico, and Henry G. Burger for permission to use material from *Ethno-Pedagogy* rev. ed., May 1971. Chapter 1 of this volume is adapted from Chapters IX–XXIV and Chapter 6 from Chapters XX–XXIV. Finally, we express our deep appreciation to Ruth Hefflebower for bringing the manuscript through its various stages of development to publishable form.

Cole S. Brembeck

Walker H. Hill
Michigan State University

PART I
From Melting Pot to Cultural Mosaic

Introduction

The idea of individual differences is rooted in educational literature and lore. Teachers-in-training are urged to recognize those psychological characteristics that set one student off from another. The child learns better, they are told, when instruction is fitted to his uniqueness as a person. Such matters as mental abilities, aptitudes, and motivations are thus regarded as individual endowments worthy of respect and available for use in the learning process.

As educators we are reasonably well tuned to the role of psychological differences in learning. We are less clear about the role of cultural endowments, and we treat them quite differently. Cultural characteristics touch us at the level of feeling, emotion, and prejudice. Instead of according them recognition and respect, as we do psychological differences, we tend to assign them "good" and "bad" designations, and we let our expectations of students be influenced by them. We tend to use cultural characteristics such as race, ethnic and national origins, language, and minority status for the purpose of sorting promising students from the unpromising. We apparently find it difficult to come at the matter of cultural diversity positively. We do not ask how cultural aptitudes might be used to support and enhance a child's classroom learning; instead, we tend to ignore or suppress these differences.

There are probably a variety of reasons why psychological and cultural characteristics elicit such different responses from educators. In the first place we know much more about the nature of psychological differences. The study of school learning has been, until recently, almost exclusively the study of educational psychology. The individual within the school setting has been the focus of scholarship and research, rather than the person as an integral part of a larger environment of family, community, race, or social class.

Second, psychological characteristics are more easily studied. Within the controlled setting of psychological laboratory and classroom, variables can be held more constant. School populations are captive subjects, readily available for testing and observation. Cultural variables, on the other hand, are more difficult to study. They spill over classroom walls and take the pursuing researcher into such mercurial institutions as the family, neighborhood, and racial group. Cultural characteristics are indeed less manageable.

Third psychological differences are less value-laden than cultural differences. They are "safer" to deal with. A teacher feels quite confident about discussing a student's psychological aptitudes, especially if he is supported by test results. Talking about cultural aptitudes, however, is quite another matter. Their relationship to how a child learns is less clear and they move a teacher from objectivity to subjectivity. In commenting publicly on a child's

3

cultural aptitudes, the teacher feels more vulnerable to attack, and in self-defense is more apt to remain quiet.

Finally, perhaps the dominant reason for treating these two types of aptitudes so differently is that we tend to regard cultural differences as transitory, on their way to being assimilated in the great American melting pot. Indeed, one function of education traditionally was to help stir the pot. Thus cultural differences did not have to be taken seriously or be reckoned with as major factors in a child's learning. They would in time go away, and meanwhile they were to be endured and put up with. In case they interfered too much with classroom learning, measures could be taken to mute their most offensive features.

Part I of this book is based on a different set of assumptions about the nature of cultural differences and their relationships to learning. Here the assumptions are that cultural characteristics (1) are as much a part of a child's endowment as psychological characteristics; (2) are influential in his learning; (3) are persistent and continuous; (4) melt very selectively and some may actually elaborate over time; and (5) are just as available for use in the improvement of teaching as are psychological characteristics.

If we can gain an appreciation of these assumptions, we may be on our way to discovering wholly new ways to teach through calling to our aid the rich and powerful cultural forces that surround us. Culture provides the larger environment in which schools are set and students learn. In Part I Henry G. Burger provides a series of explorations into different areas of this environment and opens up new vistas along these frontiers of learning.

1

Cultural Pluralism and the Schools

Henry G. Burger

The prevailing ideology in the United States with respect to ethnic differences, anthropologist Henry G. Burger points out, calls for the assimilation of all groups into a single average Yankee. History does not agree with the ideology. In practice the disintegration of older ethnic communities has caused Americans to form new groups to serve as an anchor in modern society. Cultural separatism is intensifying rather than diminishing, as evidenced by the disinclination of third and fourth generations of newcomers to blend into a standard uniform American type. What distinguishes one culture from another? Burger finds characteristic differences in value orientations in respect to such matters as cognition, affect, communication, the use of time, social organization and the sense of environmental control. He then discusses each of these with respect to how students learn and teachers teach in classrooms.

In American history there have been three different goal systems of assimilation.[1] These may be called "Anglo conformity," "melting pot," and "cultural pluralism." These three different viewpoints have appeared throughout American history, and not in any particular serial timing.

The Anglo conformity theory demanded the complete renunciation of the immigrant's ancestral culture in favor of the behavior and values of the Anglo-Saxon core group. By contrast, the melting pot idea proposed a biological merger of Anglo-Saxon people with other immigrant groups. Along with the intermarriage there would be a blending of their cultures in a new, single, native "American type." Cultural pluralism favored the preservation of the communal life and significant portions of the culture of the later immigrant groups within the context of American citizenship.

The Anglo conformity idea about immigrants was expressed by educator Ellwood P. Cubberly in 1909: "Everywhere these people tend to settle in groups . . . and to set up here their national manners, customs, and observances. Our task is to break up these groups or settlements, . . . and to implant in their children . . . the Anglo-Saxon conception of righteousness, law and order, and popular government."[2]

The melting pot ethos of a new blend was seen by a European traveler as early as 1782: "He is an American, who leaving behind him all his ancient prejudices and manners, receives new ones from the new mode of life he has embraced. . . . Here individuals of all nations are melted into a new race of men."[3]

An example of the unconscious Yankee tendency toward expecting amalgamation of every ethnic group with its own system is seen in its hyphenation approach to naming those groups. Thus, considerable discussion and reading convinces us that the layman would like to refer to a "Spanish American" rather than (as the anthropologist might) an "Hispanic." The former situation implies that the poor chap is half-way toward being assimilated, halfway toward being humanized. He is, in the melting pot analogy, half-melted. Thus the melting pot concept is approximately that of assimilating the minority into the majority.

Although cultural pluralism, has, like the other two, appeared throughout American history, its strength is relatively the latest of the three.[4] An example of the cultural pluralism approach is seen in attempts by several groups immigrating to the early nineteenth century United States to establish communal societies of their own.[5]

The foregoing three ethoses—Anglo conformity, melting pot, and cultural pluralism—have been the ideologies in the United States. But what has been the actual situation?

The Continuation of Ethnic Social Structures

History does not agree with the hope of the Apostle Paul that "there should be neither Jew nor Greek." It would seem that the melting pot has been closest to the fact in the economic sphere, Anglo conformity in the power structure, and cultural pluralism in the daily social life: "Within the ethnic group there develops a network of organizations and informal social relationships which permits and encourages the members . . . to remain within the confines of the group for all of their primary relationships and some of their secondary relationships throughout all the stages of the life cycle."[6]

According to Will Herberg, in a study of general trends in contemporary America, the disintegration of the old ethnic subcommunities has caused Americans to perceive a growing need for some new group to serve as a reference anchor in modern society.[7] The *process* of acculturation in America has been overwhelming. However, there has been little *structural* assimilation. Each racial and religious and national origin group has maintained its own network of cliques, clubs, organizations, and institutions. The interethnic contacts occur only at the secondary group level—employment and political processes.

The result has been another case of Anglo "doublethink": imagining a melting pot while grudgingly conceding some cultural pluralism attitudes. *"We have consistently failed to accept the reality of different cultures within our national boundaries.* Negroes, Indians, Spanish Americans, and Puerto Ricans are treated as though they were recalcitrant, undereducated, middle class Americans of northern European heritage instead of what they really are: members of cultural differentiated enclaves with their own communication systems, institutions, and values."[8]

Sociological consensus suggests that the cultural separatism is intensifying rather than diminishing. ". . . The American ethos is nowhere better perceived than in the disinclination of the third and fourth generation of newcomers to blend into a standard uniform national type."[9]

Further evidence is provided by a statistical study of a sample of 750 residents of Detroit. Most signs pointed to gains in the vigor and vitality of religious associations. Religion was found to be having an impact on all the other institutional systems of the community. "On the basis of such comparisons we can only conclude that differences among socioreligious groups are not declining and are not likely to decline in the forseeable future. . . . There are numerous indications that they may become more pronounced in the future. . . . Socioreligious differences are greater among members of the middle class than among members of the working class."[10] And such differentiation is only a part of the social categorization. Gordon found that the Yankee identifies himself in the following sequence: nationality (such as American); race (such as white or Amerindian); religion; national origin of self or ancestors (such as English or Spanish).[11] Even if religious *institutions* lose members, religion remains or thrives as a rallying point of informal grouping.

From Ethnic Coexistence to Ethnic Separatism

The notion that the intense and the unprecedented mixture of ethnic and religious groups in American life was soon to blend into a homogeneous product has outlived its usefulness, and also its credibility.

Tracing the emergence of a Pan-Indian movement, Robert K. Thomas considered it a reaction against the extreme pressures of industrialism: "The older civilizations were agriculturally based and in the nature of the case incorporated tribal groups as whole social units and at a leisurely, nonthreatening pace. Modern industrial civilization, through the vehicle of the bureaucratic nation-state and its institutions, demands not only the incorporation of tribal peoples but immediate incorporation and individual assimilation. Industrial civilization individuates and attacks the solidarity of the social group. . . . The first reaction of tribes under this kind of stress is the banding together of tribal groups and a widening and bolstering of this new identity in self-defense."[12]

One way to interpret the growing ethnic separatism is in terms of the concept of Alfred Kroeber that cultures tend to specialize to such an extent that they limit their own futures. Yankee culture is industrial, impersonal, and with all the other characteristics that distinguish it from the Hispanic and other elements within its borders. Thus the further industrialization and automation of life further alienates and distinguishes the ethnic minorities. The period since World War II has seen a vast increase in such cybernation; consequently, the alienation between ethnic groups has been increasing.

We cannot believe that the solution is either to reduce the automation of the Anglo part of the culture, or to automate the more personalistic ethnic minorities within that culture. Rather, we are forced to conclude that the only solution is ethnic specialization (not quite separatism) accompanied by interethnic tolerance.

One of the factors typical of Yankee pattern so rapidly developing as to be causing cleavage between Yankees and minority ethnic groups is computerization. At present, it is programmed to emphasize individualism and cognition. Yet it could emphasize sociality and affect.[13] Its fluidity now being applied to individual instruction *could* be broadened to allow for ethnic diversity and ethnic norms.

The desire for polyethnicity (rather than for melting pot) continues. An interview with 25 different organizations in the United States concerned with cultural and ethnic problems revealed that almost all favored "cultural pluralism." A somewhat typical definition was: "The right and value of diverse cultures working on the things they wished to, as long as those cultural facets did not impinge on others. The right of diverse cultures to exist side-by-side and to preserve whatever they wish as long as they did not interfere with the rights of others."[14]

The Relationship of Coexistence Policy to Schooling

The decision on melting pot or polyethnicity greatly affects the type of schooling that should be given. The question thus becomes one of providing all cultures in the U.S. with an equal *opportunity* rather than merely with equal *treatment*, as Harry Soslow has noted.[15] If we believe in melting pot, then we should teach every person the same types of skills and culture. If, however, we believe in polyethnicity, we should identify the traditional strengths of each group, cognitive, affective, and psychomotoric. Then we should notice whether the economic opportunity—which the behavioral scientist might call "ecological niches"—will remain steady, increase, or decrease. We would, according to this second doctrine, teach these specializations to each ethnic group differently as long as they will either persist or increase.

Yet the same paradox appears in both general interethnic relations and interethnic schooling policy. The more one assimilates, the more he crushes ethnic pride and specialization. The more he separates, the more he can be accused of prejudicial discrimination.

What degree of commonality must remain? We know of no sure answer, but would expect that within the United States there would generally supervene a common language and a common market. Mass communication and transportation will not be rolled back. Rather, the encouragement of ethnic diversity in such areas as vocations would, we believe, provide greater security for the single national government than the present procrustean fester.

We believe that the trend is toward polyethnicity, or cultural pluralism. We believe that time will convince more members of each ethnic minority that they cannot fully attain the core of the Anglo "style of life" (including all of its material benefits). Instead, they should proudly elaborate their own ethnic heritage, not a reactionary "back-to-the-blanket" retreat but a syncretism that enables their specialties to interweave with the complex mid-twentieth century life. The fluid, protean nature of the computer *could* facilitate such diversity—if the school establishment would accredit diversity.

Consequently, the evidence is strongly suggestive, although not conclusive, that education should train people for their ethnic "efflorescences," providing that those specialties are likely to continue in the future and that the individuals are willing to study them and do not wish to change from their traditional kin network of occupation.

In accordance with the concept of specialization, it may well be possible to teach a common core of subject matter, such as language, and then to go on and teach an ethnic speciality. This speciality need not be degrading; it may simply be traditional. It is not mere handiwork, but a cultural heritage, including great literature, human relations, and so on. Such an approach suggests that domination of the educational establishment within the ethnic geographical areas will increasingly pass to the most competent leaders of minorities.

The attitude of minority group toward control of its own schools is seen in the different terms applied by the Navajos: Apparently they feel so far away from control of the Bureau of Indian Affairs schools that they refer to them as "washingdon bi oltka," which means "Washington schools." Even the public schools on the Navajo Reservation are similarly considered lost from their control, as it would appear from their name for them: "bibagaha bi oltka" means, "little white man's schools." By contrast, the Rough Rock school, whose board of directors are themselves Navajos, is commonly called "nine bi oltka," which means "the school of the Navajo people."[16]

If, then, the cultural minorities are to play an increasing role in education, we must consider systematically the factors in which one culture may differ from another.

Ethnic Variables and Cross-Cultural Education

What distinguishes one culture from its neighbors? How do distinguishing characteristics influence the way students from different cultural backgrounds learn in classrooms? How can teachers adapt their methods in order to take advantage of these differences? In the following section we look at a number of ethnic variables found in classrooms and how they may be used through effective cross-cultural teaching.

Cognition versus Affect versus Psychomotion

Because the human intertwines brain and body, it is difficult to categorize cultural activities separately from other human activities. We use as expedient the oft-cited (but dimly substantiated) division of the human domains into cognition (the intellectual function), affect (the emotional function), and psychomotion (the motor skills function). A few special remarks about each of the domains may now be given.

Many social scientist believe that Anglo culture emphasizes *cognition* and deemphasizes affect and psychomotion, as compared with other cultures. "The demand that is being made on the schools . . . is, also, a demand that they produce a certain variety of human being—abstract, theoretical, rational, and hence, deracinated—the academic man writ large."[17] Indeed, so great is the Anglo emphasis upon cognition that one of the derogatory words used by certain minority groups about the Anglo is to call him "Bigbrain."

The amount and style of *affect* also differ among ethnicities. Because Anglo dominance structures the educational system toward cognition, the exotic-culture child is put at a disadvantage. His schooling situation is "drily" imcomplete as compared with his "better" balanced home and community. He loses interest in the classroom.

Therefore, the teacher must be willing to be emotional toward the minority child more often than toward an Anglo child; for example, by cuddling the child. If she feels uncomfortable in doing this, or if she does not yet know the child well enough to have the child's trust, she can utilize other ethnic minority people at her school. For example, a teacher in one school[18] found that an important function of the lunchroom cooks was just to provide such emotional rapport with the Hispanic children: when a child was worried about something, he would not confide in his (Anglo) teacher, but would wait until lunchtime. Not only was the cook Hispanic in culture, but she had other characteristics that resembled the child's beloved mother; for example, she wore an apron! School emphasis on cognition needs enrichment, then.

Similarly, in observing eight hours of planned, academic ceremonies at Albuquerque, New Mexico, Indian School, I noted only one highly enthusiastic event—the spontaneous singing of some Apache Amerindian songs! To non-Anglos, pure thinking is only a part of life.

Anglo culture seems to confuse *psychomotor skill* with merely manual labor like hod carrying, and so downgrades it. Most other cultures distinguish skill from toil, and award prestige at least for the former: for example, weaving and precise bodily movements in games. Young Sioux Amerinds, for example, possess

fine personal sensibility, the brilliance of their singing, the virility of their dancing, their exuberant vitality. . . . We vividly recall one occasion in which we stepped from a powwow that was distinguished by the most exciting singing and dancing, into a classroom where some well-meaning Anglo teacher was leading Amerindian children through the familiar, dreary, off-tune rendition of a nursery song. Later, members of this staff were to talk with us about what they were, condescendingly, doing for these "culturally deprived" children.[19]

It would seem that the more complex cultures, and especially the northern European cultures (including the United States), distinguish the three domains more than most other societies. They simultaneously tend to favor cognition over affect and psychomotion.

By contrast, many non-Anglo societies seek a balance of all human capabilities.

In a folk society, the child would have to master a great variety of particular bits of knowledge, concerning particular persons, topographic features, rites, skills, and so on. . . . By contrast, the typical Anglo urban school is oriented toward instilling a knowledge that is abstract, general, and in some sense "rational," and, thereby, deracinated.[20]

It is in this imbalance between the domains of learning capacity, and the irrevelance to minority living of much of the cognitive content, that we may find one explanation of ethnic minorities' disenchantment with Yankee education. For example, a study of Sioux Amerindian high schoolers suggests that many or most of those who drop out simply cannot endure the "excessively" cognitive part of high school.[21] Particularly when restricted for some minor offense from movies, town, or other affective aspects of life, they abandon the school career entirely. By contrast, most of the Sioux high school *girl* dropouts who were studied, left because they were unable to tolerate their *social* disadvantages. They felt embarrassed in ragged or unfashionable dress. But costume, too, is not directly related to intellect!

If this is the case, an obvious solution for cross-cultural teachers would be to increase affective and psychomotoric parts of education, whether by adding separate periods (devoted, say, to dance), or by incorporating them with cognition. In the second method, an instance might be a teacher's converting a purely verbal description of, say, social history at the time of the Navajo Long March into a painting class whereby students would illustrate the trek by studying and depicting the correct clothing styles, distance of average tribesmen from leaders, and range of tools carried. Thereby, non-Anglo cultures' balance could be restored.

Communication

Having discussed cognition, affect, and psychomotion, we turn to the problem of communicating.

Ethnic differences in communication show themselves in a variety of ways, including dialects, gestures, vocabulary, the social context of language and bilingualism. Let us look at these differences and their implications for teaching and learning in classrooms.

While in fact there are many dialects and other sociocultural distinctions among the inhabitants of the United States, the melting pot philosophy tends to deny them. It is suggested instead that existing dialects be used as a channel toward the goal, such as "English as a second language."

A similar tolerance concerns vocabulary involving social class. The American view of the relations between people is egalitarian; there is an avoidance of addressing people by certain polite forms, an avoidance of respectful gestures such as bowing and saluting. Other cultures, especially the Japanese, believe that this shows extreme disrespect, and threatens the very foundation of life.[22] The school need not suppress minority culture styles.

Gesturing forms also differ among ethnicities. Navajo gestures and motions are sustained, flowing, and circular, in contrast to Anglos' angular and staccato motions.[23] There are ethnic difference in eye behavior; an example is seen between Yankees and Englishmen: The proper Yankee looks straight in the eye at a person with whom he is speaking only when he wants to be very certain that he is being understood. Normally, however, the Yankee lets his gaze wander from one eye of the partner he is speaking to the other. His gaze even leaves the face of the partner for long periods.

By contrast, the Englishman, normally standing farther away, looks straight at the partner, never bobbing his head or grunting. Instead, he indicates that he understands by occasionally blinking his eyes.[24]

But again ethnic difference need not be suppressed in the name of efficiency. The facts that Anglos tend to look one another in the eye need not prevent learning by ethnicities which do not have this habit. There are still other ways of observing. The Anglo deaf, for example, are taught in part by looking at the *mouth* of a speaker. It would seem that the Amerind could be taught to look at the mouth of his teacher in classes requiring such precision, such as linguistics, and still not look her in the eye. Hence he could obey the pattern of many cultures—Amerinds, for example—to be courteous by avoiding direct eye glances.

Ethnic groups use sound differently in language. In some Amerindian groups, a perfectly accepted social visit emphasizes mere physical presence, and not necessarily speech, particularly where one has nothing new to report. Consequently, it is an acceptable social visit to come to a person's house, sit silently for half an hour, and leave still silent.[25]

For many white teachers, speaking loudly and directly is a normal cultural trait. However, Mesquaki Fox Amerindian children near "Toma, Iowa, interpret those behaviors as the teacher's being angry.[26] Again, the use of a loud voice means anger among many Amerindian groups, but may mean normality among many Hispanics. We thereby find that even loudness is not subject only to physical needs in communication.

With respect to vocabulary the "typical" unilingual Anglo six-year-old has had several years of continuous practice in hearing, via his parents and neighbors, thousands of speech patterns in the English language. He has an understanding (listening) vocabulary of about 9,000 English words and a speaking vocabulary of about 6,000.[27]

This child has learned his vocabulary in a single culture, which minimizes interference between the sectors such as child, parents, school, and community. But if we perceive the problems of communication modes within a single culture, how much more complex must they be when used between cultures, as in an interethnic teaching situation!

Language is always part of a social situation. The relationship between knowledge of a word and its social usage is seen in many studies; Eells showed that lower class children failed to identify words such as "harp." We may reasonably assume that the ghettos are not filled with people playing harps! Again, many a Puerto Rico student considers a school examination so formal as to deserve an ornate and allusive style of answer. But the Anglo teacher will often consider such a style as an attempt to conceal ignorance.[28]

As another example of the relationship between vocabulary, grammar, and social situation, we are reminded of an experiment performed by New York Medical College through the Peabody Picture Vocabulary Test. Testers found categorizable clusters of words that lower class four-year-old black children could not identify: action words like building; rural words such as bee; substantive words such as caboose.[29] Hence schools cannot teach "pure" language without considering social class and ethnic derivation.

The belief that all persons in the United States speak English is quite false. Actually, bilingualism is extensive. Approximately 11 percent of the population are *native* speakers of European languages other than English alone.[30] And even for the much larger percent who hear a non-English tongue at home, its emotional impact is great. Some years ago Margaret Mead reported the bulk of evidence then to the effect that "a basic condition of successful literacy . . . is that it should be attained in the mother tongue. Literacy achieved in any language other than the mother tongue is likely . . . to remain superficial and incomparable with the literacy of people who learned to read in the language in which their mother sang them to sleep."[31] Using that mother tongue offers rich opportunities for motivating children.

We have now seen how language, body motion, and other semiotics can differ greatly between cultures, and can be easily misinterpreted by a person of another culture. We are ready to consider the similarity and diversity between ethnic groups in the matter of use of time.

Time

Vast differences occur in ethnic attitudes toward time. These may be partially, but only partially, related to methods of subsistence. Thus, in agriculture, or at least preartificialized agriculture, the weather could not be hurried. Why, then, should agriculturists require precision or even speed-up in such matters as training children?

The impact of a differently oriented culture brings confusion. In Latin America, for example, where time is treated rather cavalierly, one commonly hears the expression, "Our time or your time?"[32] By contrast, industrialism requires that each specialist be at his station at the moment an assembly line delivers a part. Time becomes "economized" as a saleable commodity.

In Hispanic culture, the "Latino" system involved unmeticulous appointments with individuals. Transactions are more of sociability than of commodities. Thus a person may run his business by inviting people at an indefinite time and dealing with them collectively and generally rather than individually. But this system works (with a Hispano), because "people who came to do business with him also came to find out things and to visit each other." Consequently, the successful "Latino" office may often have fifteen or more people in the waiting room.[33]

The temporal differences that pervade a culture also pervade its maturing of citizens. In a simpler culture, education does not usually involve time pressure. Equipment seems to be adequate. The object of instruction, such as a fishnet, is always available, and the teachers seem always to know their subject matter. On the other hand, there may be a great deal of stereotyping, such as designating persons who are outside their tribe as "nonhuman."

In a complex culture, especially Yankee, a pupil is limited in what he may learn from the teacher by the fact that the teacher often rushes through the lessons. She also often lacks adequate equipment, teaches about things that are often remote to her and to the pupil either in space or time or both. And she teaches subjects in which she herself is weak in knowledge. "It is more difficult for a child to learn in this culture than in nonliterate cultures."[34]

Yet there are many ways to accommodate ethnic differences in a time schedule. Generally, the representatives of the culture who tend to be first or prompt should bring material that will take an indefinite amount of time. Then they will not be anxious to press those who are late or irregular. Thus, if an Anglo has made an appointment to visit a Hispanic at a certain time, such as a teacher to meet the parent of one of her Hispanic school children at a certain place and time, she should bring reading material so that she will not be angry if the other person arrives, say, 25 minutes late. We do not say that either promptness or laxness is superior. We merely suggest that "buffer" devices be used as sycretisms.

The precision of second hands correlated with a global Greenwich Mean Time is, then an illusion. Timing is determined not by the impersonal sun and stars, but by cultures. And ethnic governance increases as we turn from physical factors like time to concededly human factors like social organization.

Social Organization

The human baby is dependent on other forms (and especially a mother) for longer than any other infant animal. "Wolf babies" seem to be either mythical or irreversibly dehumanized. An equivalent dependence on one's fellows if probably true of human adults also.

Despite this vast interdependence, the value of independence is so strong among the Yankees that it pervades their educational system.

The modern school system is premised on the notion that its population is an aggregate of social atoms, among whom there are no significant or permanent linkages. . . . These social atoms begin at the same starting line and they move onward in haphazard clumps, each . . . according to its own inner strengths and motives. What each individual does in school, and later in his vocation, is an achievement—benefit only to himself and his immediate family. Contrary to this ideology is the normative system of a folk community. . . . In this system the individual may excel only when his excellence enhances the position of his brethren.[35]

Folk consensus is more prevalent in the non-Anglo cultures. Social organization begins with the family and works outward to other kin.

Kinship refers to that type of society that is based around family ties. The center or nucleus of a family will of course be the parents and the children, with aunts, uncles, and others being the more distant branch of the family. The *family* in English-speaking countries once equalled *kindred*. In northwestern Europe it includes all the people related to ego through blood or marriage, traced bilaterally and equally through both sexes to an infinite degree. Such relatives are considered measurably close or distant. If close, marriage between them is forbidden. The closest relatives are those within the nuclear family that is isolated from other members of the family as a whole. This type of grouping particularly fits the great mobility and small residences of modern America, although it is an old Anglo-Saxon form. The system produces atomism and egalitarianism. Upon marriage each individual makes a unique family. Only a part of it is the same as his closest relatives' family. He is individualized. His children inherit property equally.[36]

In such a "nuclear family" situation, there is separation, not continuity, between the generations. The Anglo—indeed the Occidental—thus enjoys a greater degree of privacy and secrecy than the members of most nonliterate societies. He excludes his children from grown-up social occasions and from much adult religious observance, and, indeed, even excludes them from the world of work.[37]

Let us contrast that Anglo-Saxonism with other systems. The English family only slightly coincides with the Spanish concept *familia*. Both terms refer to an indefinitely extended group of bilaterally traced blood relatives. In the English concept, however, relatives by marriage are vaguely and ambiguously considered kin. But the Spanish system refers primarily to patrilineal inheritance of surnames. The Anglo social organization thereby minimizes family and kin, and substitutes "rational" or "instrumental" associations, such as fellow members of one's profession. By contrast, most other cultures enlarge their social organization via kinship.

How should classrooms adapt to native social organization? Once again, we find an ethnological pattern extending from the community into the classroom. Each ethnic child is unconsciously prepared for adulthood by his own culture, although the plan does not always succeed. Probably the percent of "psychological dropouts" paces both the rigidity and the instability of the society.

We have just seen that although the United States does not push responsibility on the child, it does (following its laissez-faire tradition) seem to be "pushing the notion of individualistic competition within the framework of the school to an almost superhuman pitch." Yet, it is striking that real progress toward spreading literacy among lower class or ethnic groups has so often occurred in the context of social movements: civil rights, the Black Muslims, and, as always, the evangelistic churches.[38] Individualism alienates other traditions.

Often when a child such as the Hispanic child, from a simple culture which is based on kinship, enters the American classroom he will feel lonely because of cultural break. A teacher who encounters this situation must encourage such a child to sit by his kin as friends, rather than by assigning a seat to him arbitrarily.[39] (The teacher also should not force boys to associate with girls as they are forced in the Anglo culture, again for the same reason.)

Still another example of the effectiveness of native social organization is seen in a Korean family situation affecting a teacher. The Korean father outranks the mother. Yet an American female social worker seeking to contact the parent of a Korean boy in trouble, consulted only the mother. She was constantly disregarded. Finally, she invited the father to school with his wife, and flatteringly consulted him first and alone. Then all went well.[40]

We have tried to indicate that each culture differs in its organization of kindred and voluntary organizations. To impose the Yankee accidents onto non-Yankees violates both ethnics and efficiency. But social organization is only one more of the cultural variables. Now let us turn to another factor— differences in attitudes toward human nature.

The Goodness of Human Nature

Different cultures have divergent attitudes as to whether human nature is basically good. We may illustrate from examples familiar to the Anglo/ European world. In the Calvinistic doctrine, human nature was believed to be corrupt; in such a society, the teacher's role would be to supervise the child closely and strictly. On the other hand, progressives allow the child to have as much individuality as he is able to productively handle, for they believe that human nature is good.

A perhaps related situation is that certain aspects of personality are considered congenital, whereas others are considered teachable. In many simpler societies, for instance, one may laugh good naturedly at another person's deficiencies in skills and knowledge. Ridicule is restricted to uncouth manners and morals.[41]

A culture's "ethical" attitude affects many of its activities. For example, it intertwines with the previously discussed variable of social organization. A society believing in the goodness of fellows is more likely to value distant kin. We do not say which came first; it may be that survival requires distant friendship, and that in turn fosters the belief in personal reliability!

One example of a variance in ethics of two different cultures is that the Anglo culture emphasizes acquisitiveness for personal gain, while some Amerindians (such as the Sioux) emphasize sharing. The difference need not be steamrollered. Again we should utilize rather than attack such customs. The teacher need merely remind the Amerindian child that the sharing should first be toward his own family. Thus when the child becomes a husband receiving a paycheck, he must first pay his bills, his loans, his savings, and only then share with the people who are more distant relatives or not relatives at all.[42] Or the goal can be syncretized by advocating the learning of two sources of knowledge, both Anglo and Amerindian, to be safer than one. Or, even more obviously, the bright student should share his knowledge with his fellows by tutoring them.

Thus we have seen that attitudes toward human nature do indeed play a very important role and should be heeded by the teacher. Each society has chosen its own way of life, and if the individuals within that society survive, who are we to say whether it is right or wrong?

The Sense of Environmental Control

Historians might say that man's attitude toward the controllability of the universe depends on the modernity, the efficiency of his technology. But anthropologists might counter that the technology depends equally on his world view: A culture does not build computers unless it values objectivity, quantification, and logic. At least two factors are involved in attitudes toward the environment. Does a culture believe that events happen or are caused? And, if caused, are the causes plannable by men? We may term the first matter "transitivity," and the latter, "prometheanism."

This latter plannability factor inlcudes not only the inanimate things such as whether the clouds will deliver rain, but also animate things, such as one's fellow man. In this respect, it is the author's impression that the Yankees believe in the possibility of controlling the subhuman parts of nature, such as rain and birds, but not the human parts. By contrast, the Marxists-Communists seem to believe in the likelihood of controlling all nature.

Cultural attitudes toward causation affect the ways in which people learn. The Wolof of French West Africa, for example, believe the self to be highly limited in power, and the world to be rather magically actuated.[41] By contrast, the Yankees seem to believe so strongly in transitivity and prometheanism that they attribute to persons the problems that probably are deep in their interethnic attitudes.

Much of the sense of "environmental control" concerns one's rank in the power rule. Cross-culturally, an environmental difference will be noted. Children of certain groups, such as Mexican, black and perhaps migrant Anglo, are more likely to expect strong commands than are Anglos. Consequently, the permissive teacher will not satisfy them or gain obedience unless he gives clear orders.[44] On the other hand, Anglo children who have been reared to lax disciplinary measures will reject commands. Indeed, they themselves usually call for more independence; they want to decide for themselves and do *not* want to be led.

How do these considerations apply to schools? Schooling and the necessity for it has increased in time and in amount of required learning for the modern youngster, due primarily to (Anglo) desire to continually push ahead in hope of financial and social advancement. The payoff seems ever farther away. This fact especially harms children of the "mañana" cultures. How, then, can persons who are relatively fatalistic be made to take the thousands of investment steps, such as learning a trigonometry formula, necessary to reach the goal, such as a school diploma?

Once again we recommend that fatalism, or "futilitarianism," be reinterpreted as "determinism." The world is to be shown to such ethnics as a determined system. The student must come to class daily. But, in return, the school must impart a certain amount of utility in that one day. This pay-as-you-go philosophy is far more understandable to an "immediacy culture" than benefit that is promised to begin a decade hence. Thus, if a futilitarian student is to complete high school, he need only walk to school daily and lift his pencil. He cannot leave school as early as did his parents, however, since his generation must work in a more complicated world.

Environmental control attitudes should not be neglected by education. The school tends to train children for docility. Yet, in the white society, Amerindian children will have to assert themselves and be self-reliant. And the traditional Amerindian training, as Ruth Benedict argued, trains and requires the Indian to be independent, self-reliant, and assertive.[45] Conflict could be minimized by teaching to fit the minority's real, not "purely academic," attitudes toward environmental control.

Adolescence is in many cultures—and certainly in the Anglo culture—the prime of life in which the young man or woman feels a necessity to master a larger portion of nature. He is filled with a need for "motor omnipotence, the need for active locomotion." Yet at that very time he probably is going to high school, where he is limited in the distance he can travel, required to fit a regular schedule, and greatly limited economically. Consequently, "automobiles more often than not are stolen by the young in search of the kind of automotive intoxication.[46] One solution might, then, be for a school to offer special driving lessons to one student as a reward for good work. Or, if he already has an automobile license, it could offer the special use of an automobile, such as three hours one evening, or to an otherwise restricted area. This would be a way of meeting the tremendous interest of high school students, especially impoverished in automotive matters, instead of trying so desperately to fight against these culture-wide influences.

Another example of divergent attitudes in environmental control may be considered in a value conflict between Anglo culture which emphasizes activity to improve oneself over nature, and traditional Amerindian (for example, the Sioux) cultures. Anglos seek to improve themselves over nature; many Amerindians adjust to nature. How, then, can the school train them? The two values can be adjusted additively or otherwise harmoniously, according to Fr. John Bryde. The teacher need simply argue that the way for the Amerindians to reach the old values of survival, leisure, and adjustment to nature is by following the Anglo value of improving self *in order to acquire that time!*[47]

In this chapter we have suggested that history and practice do not agree with the prevailing ideology in the United States that all groups will "melt" into a single, average Yankee. In fact, industrialization and specialization are probably pushing us in exactly the opposite direction. Cultural separatism is intensifying rather than diminishing.

Since cultural pluralism seems to be the mode in our society we then asked: What characteristics *do* distinguish one culture from another? We have discussed cultural differences in cognition, affect, and psychomotion; communication; attitudes toward time; social organization; in attitudes toward the goodness or badness of human nature, and the sense of environmental control. Perhaps more importantly we have suggested how these cultural differences may be used in the classroom to enhance the learning of ethnic-background students. Too frequently in the past these characteristics have caused these students to become alienated from schools with a predominantly Anglo culture. Now it is important to see ethnic characteristics as powerful resources for learning, since they spring from the student's primary culture. Rather than being denied in the classroom, they can and should be used to promote educational achievement.

Part II
The Challenge of Diversity and Conflict

Introduction

In Part I Henry Burger presented evidence of the continuing persistence of ethnic characteristics, the failure of the melting pot to melt, and the need for teachers to understand and appreciate subcultural differences.

In Part II we reach into four quite different geographic regions for experiences in providing schooling in a variety of cultural settings, in order to gain both historical and sociological perspectives. First we look at the case of Hawaii, called by Ralph Stueber "a natural laboratory in which to study cultural factors in educational change." Then we travel to New Zealand, where John Watson reviews for us a quarter-century of experience in providing schooling for Maori children. Next we visit three Asian countries, in which Cole Brembeck speculates on the influence of rising enrollments on the values of schools and the larger community around them. Finally, we return to the United States, where Thomas Pettigrew and Particia Pajonas report what research says about the comparative values of homogeneous and heterogeneous schooling. From these cross-cultural comparisons emerge the central issues involved in the assimilation vs separatism debate.

Cultural diversity implies diversity of values. It also implies the possibility of conflict among diverse values. A cultural mosaic consists both of discrete elements and the lines which form their boundaries and join them together. These lines, if we may borrow geological terms, may be thought of as fault lines where frictions take place and pressures build up. Sometimes small pressures may be released by minor accommodations on each side. Moderate pressures may be released in moderate tremors. But strong pressures may result in violent dislocations.

Schools, as social institutions, tend to be located at the convergence of cultural fault lines. There is almost a built-in susceptibility to cross-cultural pressure and conflict. In Part II we examine the anatomy of this conflict and suggest ways by which the schools may handle it constructively.

The earlier concept of complete assimilation was an ideal never fully attained. The melting pot did not melt completely. Cultural separatism is also an ideal which likely will not be realized in full. Society will continue to have sectors where assimilation is obvious; it will have other areas where clear separatism exists. Perhaps a more reachable goal is that of trying to provide within a pluralistic society for both separate cultural identity and cohesion among subcultures of the mosaic. Such a society will encourage the cultural essences of each group to flourish within the mosaic; at the same time it will provide the cement which holds the total mosaic together. That goal provides a challenge of immense excitement for the schools.

What themes historically run through the efforts of schools to educate minority populations? Here are some of the themes that emerge in the four chapters of Part II. First, there is the effort of one subculture, the dominant one, to provide the schools, while the parents of another subculture, the

21

minority one, provide the children. This separation of educational control from the consumers of education is a predictable part of the structure of cross-cultural education.

Second, there are the efforts of the dominant group to provide minorities with the tools of assimilation, for example the language of the dominant group, its history, lore, hopes, and aspirations.Third, there is the resistance of minorities to assimilation and their remarkable genius for preserving continuity in their cultural stream. Fourth, there is the lack of fit between the child's home values and those of the school.

These children, who stand between the traditional values of their parents and the alien ones of the school, are called upon to become cultural bridges—no easy task for even the most pliable young. Then there is the crucial issue of public policy for educating minorities. Should policy be in the direction of complete assimilation? Complete separatism? Should it provide for some of each, and if so, in what areas? These issues are amply illustrated by Stueber's examination of the case of Hawaii and Watson's analysis of Maori education in New Zealand.

Everywhere, previously unschooled groups are participating in education in increasing numbers. What are the social consequences of having in the schools large minority groups whose cultural values are frequently at odds with the traditional elites in education? Chapter 4 poses questions such as: To what kinds of conflicts does this diversity give rise? How does it restructure social and political power? How does it affect what is learned in school and how?

Finally, there is the issue of the role of the school in carrying out public policy for the education of minorities. This is the big issue for all who work in schools or who are otherwise concerned with them. Public policy on the education of minorities in the United States is now legally based in integration and assimilation. At the same time, forces arguing for separatism are strong and points of conflict are all about. In this charged atmosphere attention to the circumstances under which children learn best is apt to be diverted. It is this crucial situation which Pettigrew and Pajonas examine in the concluding chapter of Part II. The challenge of diversity is sharpest in the classroom where students and teachers confront each other across the diversity of cultures.

Cultural pluralism presupposes the need to manage differences constructively within an environment marked by tolerance, appreciation, and the means of conflict resolution. These chapters examine this necessity from the perspective of schools and what they can do about it.

2

Schools and Cultural Assimilation

Ralph Stueber

The author, a student of Hawaiian educational history, traces the development of Hawaiian schools through successive stages of the Islands' history, describes the functions of schools in the lives of the American, native Hawaiian, and Oriental populations, and focuses on their segregating and assimilating functions. He shows that, with industrialization in the modern period, there has come a large measure of assimilation of Hawaii's peoples, in which the schools have played a central role.

Hawaii provides a natural laboratory in which to study cultural factors in educational change. Studies of schools which have been enveloped historically in a rich variety of cross-cultural forces can contribute to our knowledge of how schools might serve as an integrating and ameliorating factor in reducing the social tensions and conflicts which inevitably develop in a society where the young are being inducted into a culture alien to their parents. These studies can also contribute to our knowledge of how schools might be used to protect and perpetuate a cultural heritage, to blunt the forces of cultural change, and to prevent the intermingling and synthesis of new cultural forms.

Education is generally defined within a single cultural context. As a form of social action, it has been defined as "a function of a particular society at a particular time and place in history; . . . rooted in some actual culture and [expressing] the philosophy and recognized needs of that culture."[1] But in a cross-cultural setting education can also be defined as the process through which individuals are helped not only to become a part of the cultural pattern with which they are most closely in touch, but to learn to avail themselves of the potential experiences within a cross-cultural setting, how to integrate these experiences, and thus become participant in and creator of a new culture.[2] Hawaii's cross-cultural setting produced schools reflecting both definitions in varying degrees at different times in History.

In telling the story of schools and cultural assimilation in Hawaii, the play of cultural forces that gave shape to her system of universal education will come to be known. Equally important, the impact of universal education in changing the nature and composition of these cultural forces will also come to be known. This requires searching into the value systems out of which education gains its direction. The cross-cultural milieu in the Islands did not provide a common set of values according to which all schooling was conducted.

If the educational historian is to get at the truth about the functions schools were expected to carry out, he must study education within the broad spheres of government, economics, family life, religion, and language. What is undertaken, then, in relation to the larger concern of schooling and cultural assimilation, is the narration of the ways in which schools in time enlarged and modified the particular cultural context they reflected and thus contributed to the gradual development of a richly varied though common way of life in the Islands that is judged "American."

The fact that integration and assimilation of diverse peoples into a more homogeneous milieu leaves old-world cultural ties only to memory does not discount the importance of the transplanted cultural enclave in providing the basis for a just and successful assimilation. Ethnic identification continues to be a characteristic way for people to form social groups long after old-world cultural ties become broken.

The schools' role in striking a balance between the reduction or perpetuation of ethnic solidarity is a vital one. Those who believed that Hawaii could become a unified community, either through stamping all immigrants as well as the native Hawaiians into the cultural pattern of the old white Anglo-Saxon Protestant stock, or by allowing the assemblage of peoples to keep their indigenous and old-world cultures intact, failed to recognize a feature of American assimilation. It has not been the process of making one people conform to the standards of another, but rather the process of helping people come together to form a new standard, to become mutually valuable and attractive to each other, and yet to retain their separate identity in many different ways.

The History of Hawaii's Cultural Assimilation

That Hawaii became the fiftieth American state is evidence that the governing forces in the assimilation of the Islands' peoples sprang from an American community. The American Protestant missionaries and their descendants turned planter and industrialist, set this direction for cultural development long before the American government, through annexation, declared that American cultural resources in Hawaii were to be the model or standard in the task of "Americanizing" the Islands.

Like the ancient Hawaiians who had migrated to the Islands from the South Pacific a millenium earlier, the Americans, Japanese, Chinese, Koreans, Filipinos, Puerto Ricans, and Europeans also carried with them to the Islands their language, tools, bodies of knowledge, and their value systems. Of these immigrants, the Americans were the most favored in the sense that their cultural characteristics were kept intact, widely acquired by others, and accepted as having the most prestige. Collectively these factors contributed to making the Americans an elite group.

Three Communities

For the purposes of setting down briefly the order in which the dominant cultural characteristics of this elite group took root in Hawaii, and of indicating the basic orientation of this elite group at different periods of its history in the Islands, three different American communities may be identified.

The first community was organized around the American Protestant missionary effort and may be referred to as the Community of the Righteous. The second community evolved out of the first, acquired a broader range of motives and a larger membership, and, because it was strongly governed by the pursuit of earthly treasures, it may be referred to as the Community of the Rich. The third American community broke through the protective social, racial, and economic walls which the earlier communities had drawn around themselves and spread the resources of American culture broadly throughout the Islands' peoples. This community may be referred to as the Community of Revolt; it was also the Community of Assimilation.

The elite that governed the Community of the Righteous was propelled to Hawaii by a thrust of American religious imperialism. Guided by the doctrines of Christian stewardship and disinterested benevolence, this religious and intellectual elite was instrumental in establishing a system of churches and schools, Western land laws, a constitutional monarchy; in expanding a capitalist economy and setting into operation a social philosophy in which a paternalistic relationship between the missionary and Hawaiian was central.

Religious motives remained the central concern in the mission-connected American community until the stimulus of land ownership, advances in sugar milling technology, and trade relations with the United States culminated in the Reciprocal Trade Treaty of 1876. During the course of these events a number of the original missionaries and many of their descendants joined together with representatives of the defunct American whaling interests in Hawaii and other speculators and investors to build the Islands' sugar economy.

By the turn of the century those who controlled the plantation system also controlled the Islands and formed the nucleus of the Community of the Rich. Annexation was the result of American secular imperialism bent upon securing American military needs in the Pacific and upon halting the Japanization of Hawaii that was allegedly taking place. Annexation was also brought about to protect Hawaii's first growing plantation economy and because the Islands' schools were judged by the American Congress to be capable of assimilating the Orientals into American culture.

The stimulus of profits set off a worldwide search for plantation laborers that came to focus primarily on China, Japan, and the Philippines. But laborers were also brought in from Korea, India, the islands of the South Pacific, the Azores, Puerto Rico, and Europe. Under the command of a white oligarchy, tempered by the doctrine of benevolence, a system of industrial paternalism wove human and natural resources of the Islands together into an enterprise which produced great wealth for the stewards of the Islands.

World War II released forces in Hawaii's society that elevated a middle class elite to power, replacing the prewar oligarchy. This new elite no longer drew its membership solely from Caucasian ranks. Instead, ethnic groups were represented roughly in proportion to the length of time each group had been in the Islands.

Under the guidance of this newly emerging leadership class, unionization of Hawaii's labor force took place rapidly at the close of the war. Through the Democratic party, the new leadership broke the monopoly of territorial political power held by Republicans from the time of annexation. Paternalism was rejected and in its place there came into being a vigorous social democracy. Ethnic lines became less significant, especially after the Islands' Japanese escaped from beneath the veil of suspicion that had hung over them almost from the time of arrival of Japanese in the Islands. The economy diversified and expanded greatly, giving range and power to the middle class in the Islands equal to that held by the middle class on the mainland. The capstone to American community building efforts, begun in the early part of the nineteenth century, came with statehood in 1959.

These in brief were the major events along the way to securing the dominance of American culture in Hawaii. In the process the uniracial, traditional society of the indigenous Island people, exposed to outside cultural forces increasingly after 1820, was transformed into a multiethnic, polyglot society.

In that society, which extended roughly from the 1880s to World War II, members of each ethnic group clung to the traditional forms of their own ancestral culture and language. But the schools laid a basis for the transformation of this society, and war catalyzed the process of change. Intermarriage created a rapidly growing new racial type, and English, or an Island dialect of English, became the mother tongue of Island children. Ethnic identification continued after the war as an important basis for social grouping, but throughout Hawaii ran increasingly broader currents of common identity based upon occupational and interest lines which crossed ethnic lines. Out of a static, feudal-like social structure of yesteryear, through a phase of striking cultural and linguistic diversity, producing tension and conflict, there emerged by the 1960s a dynamic, secularized, plural society geared to world markets and to national and supranational politics.

The Schools' Response

The response of the majority of Hawaii's schools to these cultural factors is best described in terms of two rather distinct cycles. In the first, the interplay of cultural factors to which schools responded and contributed was between those portions of Hawaiian culture which had survived the physical, psychological, and social devastation which the first penetration of the *haole*[a] had caused, and the missionary and his way of life. This first cycle extended roughly from 1820 to 1900. During this time span Hawaii's educators created the systems of schools which carried education through its second cycle—the period during which Hawaii served its apprenticeship for statehood as a United States territory.

[a] The term *haole* is used extensively throughout this study. Originally the Hawaiians called the white men who arrived in the islands in 1778 and after, haoles. As more white men came to Hawaii, haole came to designate all white men and their ways. To do something in the manner of the whites was to do it the haole way or haole style. As haoles achieved economic, political, and social advantages of which Hawaiians, and later Orientals, were often resentful, the term connoted resentment as well.

Having carried the dwindling remnant of Hawaiians into the framework of haole paternalism, and helping them accommodate themselves to the increasingly complex social and cultural forces that swirled about them, the schools began the second cycle. Having assimilated the Hawaiians to a considerable degree, the schools then had to face the immensely greater task of assimilating the Orientals.

While the elites of the Community of the Righteous and the Community of the Rich charted the course of these two cycles, they did not as a general rule send their own children to schools involved with that assimilating function. Rather, the children of the elite attended "select" or "standard" schools, meaning that they went to schools which were defined as transmitters and complementors of the culture of the parent stock, rather than as agencies helping children become participants in a culture alien to their parents. The total educational results of these two cycles were the basis upon which the post-World War II social revolution was sustained and the achievement of the Community of Islanders gained. Statehood coincided in time with the shift in division of Island schools (according to function) from educating an alien group in one and an American group in the other, to the division of schools according to the features that fell within the American cultural context. Given this outline—and the warning that it is too neat and simple to enlist the total confidence of the writer—it is now possible to examine more specific instances of the ways in which schools met the challenge of cultural assimilation.

How the Schools Met the Challenge

The American missionary thrust was synonymous with Hopkinsian utopianism, a mixture of Protestant evangelism and resurgent Calvinist theology that was widespread in New England in the latter part of the eighteenth century. With a zeal comparable to that of a sixteenth century Spanish mystic, the young New England clergymen took as their mission the conversion of the non-Christian along the moral lines of New England. They believed themselves entrusted with divine ordinances in their mission abroad, including Hawaii. Their instructions were ". . . to aim at nothing short of covering those islands with fruitful fields and pleasant dwellings, and schools and churches" and to raise up ". . . the whole people to an elevated state of Christian civilization. . . ."

After three decades in the Islands, the American Board of Commissioners for Foreign Missions could report some successes in the task of molding the Hawaiians in the image of the haole missionaries. Repeatedly the American Board described a kind of genetic relationship between New England and Hawaii, noting that as the Pilgrim fathers had made New England resemble England so the missionaries would make Hawaii to resemble New England.

The missionaries were also instructed to entertain a solitary dread of division among themselves. "you are one; one in purpose, one in affection, in action one" they were told. Setting themselves "as a city on a hill that could not be hid" and working in the belief that God had divided people into two classes, one to rule over the other for the good of all, the missionaries then moved down into the valley of the heathen. This particular concept of their community and its relationship to the Hawaiians lay at the heart of attempts to assimilate the Hawaiians and later the Orientals.

The first company of missionaries moved into a religious vacuum. The Polynesian *Kapu* system, the keystone in the arch of Hawaiian culture, was in shambles. Hawaiian *Kahunas* were being discredited; their old idols had been burned and their temples destroyed. Impressed with the white man's artifacts, the Hawaiian people and their chiefs eagerly sought out the haole's priests. The missionaries took these events as evidence of divine intervention in their behalf.

Fed by haole guns and ammunition, the machine of war under Kamehameha I had united the Islands under a single kingdom. But physically and culturally Hawaii lay a wasteland upon the missionary arrival. The greed of Yankee sandalwood traders as well as of Hawaiian chiefs, when coupled with haole diseases, contributed further to the collapse of Hawaiian culture.

To stamp out sin and bring Hawaiians into the province of God, these God-glorifying, militant, selfless men depended upon the overarching authority of the Bible as the ultimate measure of all human experience and set out to make it universally available to the Hawaiians. This required literacy and from their city on the hill the missionaries began a most remarkable educational experiment . Here was the historical root of Hawaii's system of universal education. Later, the commercial and industrial revolution, and the advent of political democracy, gave further support to universal education, but the American missionaries provided the foundation to which that support was added.

By the time the missionaries arrived, Hawaiians, and in particular the chiefs in the harbor villages, had had four decades of contact with English-speakers. A few Hawaiians undoubtedly spoke English with fluency, but Hawaiian was the first language of all Hawaiians. The missionaries did not establish themselves in the commercial harbor areas; nor did they intend to proselytize only those who understood English. Consequently they undertook an intense effort to create a written language for the Hawaiians and to translate the Bible and other literature appropriate to their concerns into Hawaiian.

In this process much of the old poetic and religious symbolism which had given meaning to the Hawaiian's life was excluded from the written language. At the same time new concepts drawn from the life patterns of New England were added to Hawaiian. The biblical culture, as it were, which had evolved for centuries in the West, was grafted and fused with Polynesian oral traditions, also the product of centuries. Here then was a major effort in assimilation which critics later took to be a barrier to assimilation rather than an aid. It was not until 30 years of educational effort had been made by the missionaries that Hawaiians began to demand that they be incorporated into the English "writing culture."

Having created a written language and translated appropriate literature into that language, the missionaries, nevertheless, did not entertain the concept of offering the Hawaiians a predominantly literary and academic schooling. In order to regenerate the whole society the mission depended upon preachers, teachers, doctors, mechanics, farmers, printers, and binders. It was a Board rule that all be married before leaving New England, and mission wives were as diligent and often more effective at working among the Hawaiians.

Although they had a beckoning ideal, the missionaries had no tested procedures to indicate how to go about their task. The educational programs they carried out suggest that demonstrating the practical arts and conducting the study of science and literature were as important to them as working out theological proofs. In many respects these hardy New Englanders represented forerunners of President Harry S Truman's Point Four Program.[3]

Early Education

The first students in mission schools were the Hawaiian adults. Through their enthusiasm to learn to read from the *Pi-a-pa,* an eight-page primer, and to then become involved with more substantive materials, Hawaii became a literate Island Kingdom within a decade. Efforts at schooling the "30,000 children all of whom lie entirely at our disposal—completely in our hands" were begun after 1830 generally.

Calvinists had always believed that for a person to feel better it was first necessary to help him feel worse. A major requirement as they saw it was to curb the natural inclinations and playful enthusiasms of the Hawaiian children and teach them restraint, industriousness, and the value of time, and above all a sense of guilt. These teachings stood in marked contrast to the child-rearing practices of the Hawaiians, even taking into account that social disorganization was taking a toll in family practices.

The Hawaiians, by comparison, were an earthy lot, adjusted historically to a bountiful environment that required little by way of laying up stores for the future. They practiced a form of communal living in which food, shelter, and sexual affections were shared more freely than anything the missionaries could accept, given their own sensitivity to the privacy of property and persons. To come of age in old Hawaii required mainly that young children were fed, protected against physical dangers, and kept out from under foot. Here were genuine obstacles in the way of assimilation.

To be judged successful in its work, the mission had to provide evidence that at least some Hawaiians were acquiring new values and outward behaviors and learning those skills that would qualify them for membership in the Community of the Righteous. Missionaries looked upon themselves and their children as a source of moral and cultural capital and guarded against unwise and wasteful investment with extreme care. Conceiving of themselves as standards to be followed and emulated, they ranked and classified schools according to the degree of moral rectitude considered possible of achievement at each level, given the resources with which the mission had to work.

Assimilation, then, was not conceived of as being fostered best by mixing all of Hawaii's children together in a common school experience, as New England's Horace Mann was advocating at the time. Although the government systems of schools which the mission had established by the 1840s resembled in some way Mann's ideal, common schools were designed for the mass of common people and not to be attended in common by all children.

Types of Schools

Government schools were divided into: (1) vernacular schools for Hawaiian commoners, taught by Hawaiian teachers; (2) select vernacular schools, for Hawaiian youth who showed special promise, taught by missionaries; (3) select English schools, for Hawaiian children whose families could afford the special tuition and considered English a valuable asset, taught by haoles many of whom were missionary descendants after midcentury; (4) a select English school for the children of chiefs, taught by missionaries; and (5) an English school for children born to a Hawaiian mother and haole father.

Independent schools were generally select schools because their clientele was generally from more advantaged circumstances and because instruction was handled by a haole. Punahou was the school begun in 1841 to allow missionaries to educate their children in the Islands rather than send them back to New England for a proper education. After 1839 French Catholics began to develop schools, and they were able not only to have government schools conducted according to principles of Catholic religion and education but could receive government aid for their select independent schools. In this they simply followed the example set by the American Protestants. By comparison, Catholic influences over the shaping of Hawaiian education were never as great as Protestant influences, and the Catholic influence reached its strength in the twentieth century.

Differences between independent and government schools and between select and common schools in terms of specific programs, resources, and objectives were clearly distinguishable. Clearly at one end of the spectrum stood the elite school of the Community of the Righteous, Punahou. By the 1870s this school could prepare a student for successful professional education at Yale, Harvard, or other prominent American universities and colleges. At the other end of the spectrum was the government common which, spread out along the Island chain, enabled the Hawaiian child to learn the three R's plus some music and geography and to learn to be law abiding and respectful to authority.

Between these extreme ends of the educational spectrum were scattered the other types of schools mentioned. While not all Punahou students were expected to go on to college, they were all assumed to be preparing for supervisory or administrative posts, some form of commercial endeavor, or a profession. These were all leadership roles. In the 1840s, for example, Punahou undertook to prepare its students for this leadership role with considerably fewer than a total of 100 students covering the entire range from the first year to graduation. A the same time there were well over 300 government common schools with a total enrollment of 18,000 children. The select schools varied in number and had a student population comprising at various times from 10 to 20 percent of the total number of children in schools. In Honolulu it was not unusual that half the total school population attended independent schools.

Teachers

The kinds and degrees of competencies of teachers spread out over a broad range. Select school teachers were haoles whose education was generally vastly superior to that of the Hawaiian teachers in the government common schools. Where haole children had haole teachers and Hawaiian children had Hawaiian teachers, the differences between teacher and pupil were differences of degree more than of kind. This was especially so if the mother tongue of both teacher and pupil was the language of instruction. Where Hawaiian children had haole teachers who taught in Hawaiian, the gap between the child and teacher was not as great as when the Hawaiian student had a haole teacher who taught in English. Exceedingly few, if any, haole children ever had Hawaiian teachers, whereas till this day Hawaiian children at the independent Kamehameha Schools have virtually all haole teachers.

A persistently critical problem in educating Hawaiians—according to the missionary conception of making Hawaiians become like them—was the shortage of teachers who reflected in the classrooms the standards of thought, behavior, and language usage they wanted children to acquire. Given this general conception of teacher qualifications, haole teachers were generally considered superior to Hawaiian teachers, and since it was exceedingly rare for a school staff to be made up of haoles mixed with Hawaiians, schools with haole teachers were considered superior schools.

This commitment to haole standards yielded a situation in which not only Hawaiian students were constantly judged by standards of another culture, but Hawaiian teachers as well. It was, of course, possible for Hawaiian teachers to reach Hawaiian children (especially if the language of instruction was the mother tongue of both) in ways that haole teachers were unable to because of cultural barriers.

After 1854 a movement was begun gradually to convert the vernacular schools into English schools. This meant that children for at least one generation would begin their studies in a foreign language and that Hawaiian would have to be learned and practiced at home if students were to remain in touch to some degree with their parents. It also meant that one of the most significant qualifications for teaching was competency in English and in teaching English as a foreign language. The select schools, and especially Punahou, set the standard, and the English common schools struggled to approximate that standard.

Linguistic complications arose not only out of the process of transforming Hawaiians into English-speakers but out of the development of pidgin English as a lingua franca among plantation workers brought into Hawaii in increasing numbers after 1860.

The accomplishments of this whole range of schooling varied widely. One notable outcome resulted from the missionaries' belief in teaching by example as well as precept. Their agricultural enterprises and shop activities, developed in conjunction with their schools and churches, gave them a foothold in Hawaii's economy and weakened their ties with the American Board as their supporting agency. Joined first by Catholics and then by Mormon and Anglican in missionary activity, the American Protestants after the 1870s were not unique in striving to help young Hawaiians become self-reliant, punctual, and industrious, and to value time and leave behind "unrestrained, boisterous, contentious, and senuous behavior."

The Economy

By the 1870s the Hawaiians had undergone three generations of exposure to the haole. The combined effect of the commerical and missionary groups ground relentlessly at the traditional mode of life of the Hawaiians. Many were able to make some adjustment to the trading, whaling, and agricultural economies, and to cope with the Western political forms woven into the Hawaiian monarchy, because of the education they had received. But at the same time Hawaiians were also taught to follow haole leadership and acknowledge the superiority of haole ways.

In 1848 missionary Amos Cooke wrote prophetically that, like the Jews in Egypt, the Americans in Hawaii multiplied rapidly but seemed destined to inherit the land rather than to be led out. However, it was sugar rather than religion that was the most substantial factor in this inheritance.

In 1872 capital investments in sugar production amounted to only four million dollars. Shortly after the turn of the century, investment stood at eighty-five million dollars, and by 1929 investments were estimated to be between $150,000,000 and $175,000,000. The center of this industry was Honolulu, and from there the control and direction radiated to the outer islands, affecting virtually every aspect of Island life. The authority of science and technology, the business and labor management know-how and the motives for profit replaced the authority of the Bible, the evangelism of the missionary, and the motives to save souls. The missionary-planter turned planter-industrialist by the end of the century and became the central figure in the haole community.

Motivated by the dizzy heights to which their worldly successes suddenly rose, the haole leadership drew the community together on this American cultural frontier around their loyalties to their tradition in Hawaii, around an increasing militancy for Americanism and mixed fear and hostility toward the Japanese in the Islands.

The plantation system the elite built was a social and political structure as well as an economic one. By 1900 18,272 Portuguese, 25,767 Chinese, and 61,111 Japanese had been drawn to Hawaii, primarily to provide the labor needs of the plantations. The "pure" Hawaii population had dwindled to a mere 29,799, although there were hopeful signs that a part-Hawaiian population would in time flourish. There were almost 10,000 in 1900. Excluding the Portuguese, the haole population numbered 8,544 or 7.7 percent of the total population. The haoles controlled the land, the government, the plantation system, and the schools; and between 1900 and 1941 they maintained that control.

The Hawaiians became passive spectators to affairs in the Islands between haoles and Orientals. Shoved one way by the haole in his course toward securing domination over the Islands and keeping Orientals in their place, and shoved another way by the Orientals in their attempt to do more in establishing a new way of life than was possible under plantation conditions, the Hawaiians were taken up increasingly with attempts to escape into the past. To be sure, through the acceptance of their sports, music, dance, and food, as well as of their generous nature and habits of hospitality, the Hawaiians could feel that they were an integral part of the life in the Islands. However, these were not the cultural traits that were determining the fate of the society. In the things that counted, the Hawaiians were not the haoles' equals.

The Orientals, in spite of lowly peasant birth, would eventually force the haoles to deal with them as equals. Out of their own cultural enclave, especially out of their remarkable family system, they would gain the strength to get an education against great obstacles, to make their contribution to Island culture, and at the same time learn to identify broadly and intimately with other Island peoples. The channel to influence, power, and equality that was kept open the widest was the channel of education.

The Conception of Public Education

While motives changed among the haole elite from religious to secular concerns, they preserved the impulse for mass education. The territorial government placed the government school systems directly under control of the territorial governor's office and thus provided Island educators with a new and more powerful authority. In the face of the flood of Oriental children entering schools between 1900 and 1920, the Department of Public Instruction maintained its compulsory attendance law, insisted that all instruction be in English and that pidgin be replaced by standard English, and gave first priority to "Americanizing" all Hawaii's youth. Until 1920 the pattern of education that had evolved prior to annexation was continued without major alterations. The Federal Bureau of Education survey of Hawaiian schools in that year changed radically the course of public education.

Until 1920 public education was conceived almost completely in terms of what would now be called an elementary school education. Like the missionaries of a century earlier, the federal commissioners conceived of education in broad social terms. Recognizing the plantation system for what it was, and the school system for what it was not equipped to do, the survey recommended sweeping improvements in all aspects of Island education. With an adequate school system "there would disappear from the minds of men in Hawaii the thought that the great enterprises of the Islands are dependent upon successive waves of cheap, ignorant, illiterate, alien laborers who stick to their jobs only through fear of want and through inability to do anything else."[4]

The major recommendations in the survey were for establishing secondary schooling on a broad basis, for revising the existing curriculum to include a heavy emphasis upon vocational education in order to prepare for the replacement of alien labor by domestic labor, for curbing the Japanese language school system, for greatly improving the quality of teacher education programs, and for expanding the government select school system substantially.

Guided by the recommendations of the survey and assisted greatly by a succession of able school superintendents, Governor Wallace R. Farrington transformed the public school system during the 1920s. The major efforts were directed toward the improvement of the common or nonselect schools which after the mid 1920s were classified as nonstandard schools.

At the time of the federal survey only 2 percent of the high school age Island youth were in high schools, but in a remarkable spurt of school development this figure rose by 1930 to almost 50 percent. The drive for secondary school education continued throughout the 1930s and 1940s until Hawaii came to lead the nation in the number of high school age youth who were actually enrolled in school.

At least three major factors were involved in this sudden expansion in secondary education prior to World War II:

1. The Oriental communities saw in education their one chance for improved status, acceptance as Americans, and economic security. The Oriental family structure, the traditional respect for learning, and a high degree of adaptability, all contributed to the remarkable success Orientals had in taking advantage of education.
2. Educational practices and objectives were modified to fit a much broader clientele, to interest students in schooling, and to help them and their parents see the value of extended attendance.
3. A strong corps of well trained and dedicated teachers developed, who were given leadership in part by an energetic, articulate, and scholarly group of progressive educators who both understood and applied much of the educational philosophy of John Dewey.

Progressive educational ideas took hold strongly after 1920 as Island social problems became the organizing centers of the curriculum. The traditional academic and classical approach to schooling was greatly supplemented by efforts to develop in schools a sense of communal morale. Extracurricular activities, expansive lunch programs, and health and recreation programs were given much attention for the sole purpose of bringing Island youth into closer personal relationships than were possible in formal classrooms. A the heart of Island progressivism was the principle that American culture and Island community life could become inseparable.

By 1940 there was increasing evidence that the nonstandard schools were not radically different from the standard schools. Hawaii had moved forward to becoming a first rate, socially mobile American community rather than remaining a socially stratified, colonial-like American dependency. The implementation of the federal survey recommendations had greatly reduced the disparity in educational achievement between haole and Oriental students. Island industrialists gradually accepted the idea of adjusting the industry to depend upon domestic labor. The schools had taught that the labor force should insist upon American Standards in wages and benefits to some degree, but the Japanese press probably did more to help labor learn lessons in human dignity, social action, and democracy "American style."

The federal survey also stimulated the development of government select schools, and by 1930 a system of such select schools including kindergarten through twelfth grade had been created by the Department of Public Instruction. The focal point of the system was Honolulu, although each of the other islands had at least one select elementary school.

This system came to be named the English Standard School system. The choice of that name revealed certain attitudes toward "pidgin" English and school standards that bear looking into. In effect, the haole community considered the nonstandard schools pidgin schools rather than English schools, and as schools that did not meet the standards of American schools. To create an English Standard School system was, therefore, to create a system of American public schools, as Americanism was understood and practiced in the Islands in the 1920s.

While the nonstandard schools admitted all Island youth without qualification as to English-speaking capability and quickness in the academic procession, the standard schools admitted students on the basis of oral English ability. This gave the children who spoke standard English as their mother tongue an obvious advantage and, therefore, it was no surprise that the standard schools appeared to be a quasi-private system primarily for haoles.

The English standard schools never enrolled more than 10 percent of the total public school enrollment, but they provided sufficient room for children whose parents could not afford to or did not want to send their children to Punahou and yet did not want their children in "pidgin" schools attended mainly by Orientals. The function of the standard school was to protect and perpetuate the language and culture of the haole group, but there were at least four significant features of this segregated school system that need to be noted:

1. Children were not segregated on racial lines; Oriental children were admitted increasingly during the 1930s and 1940s.
2. The schools were never considered more than a temporary measure. They would in a sense be abolished as segregated schools when their standards were achieved by the nonstandard schools.

3. Teachers in the standard schools were haoles until late in the 1930s and then a few nonhaoles were placed in these schools.
4. These schools served to attract the middle class into the public schools and thereby increased the support base of government schools. Monies for teachers' salaries and equipment were equally distributed among standard and nonstandard schools.

It is interesting to note that the Punahou Mothers' Association took the initiative in helping standard schools organize Parent-Teacher Associations. The predominantly haole middle class could not afford Punahou and they could not have been accommodated if they had been able to. The English standard schools in a sense became middle class Punahous.

The Japanese Community

In its struggle to win acceptance and a place among the rest of the Islands' peoples, the Japanese community never completely accepted haole status and prestige. This was, in large measure, the result of the size and cohesion of the Japanese group. Their enclave perpetuated the high esteem with which they held their own way of life. Buddhist temples, Shinto shrines, tea houses, formal gardens, a Japanese language press, Japanese language schools, and a developing Japanese professional and business community, all served to give stability and continuity to the Japanese sense of pride and exclusiveness.

Once Japanese children were old enough to attend the public schools, they became caught in a cultural tug of war. When they reached school age they were exposed progressively to the features of the haole community, which contained all the attributes of a complete and different way of life. While the initial and major contact with haole ways was through the schools, the playground, theatres, commercial houses, the major newspapers, and the general community mores completed the exposure to a different pattern of life. Exposed to this strange new environment in which other children teased and ridiculed their old-country ways, Japanese school children quickly began to question their belief in parental infallibility which their home life had nurtured.

In a world beyond the home, Japanese school children quickly adopted an article of American faith, i.e., what is done by most of the people is the right and only thing to do. Here was a major source of conflict between the first and second generation and a cause of considerable personal disorganization among the members of the second generation. Japanese language schools were established as a means of easing the tension and slowing the process which was culturally separating children from their parents.

Between the time when the immigrant Japanese looked upon Hawaii as a temporary home and the time when a majority accepted the fact that they would remain permanently in the Islands in order to be with their children and grandchildren, the Japanese language schools underwent a change in basic purpose. Where formerly these schools prepared Japanese children for reentry into Japanese society, they changed their orientation to provide continuity between generations as the life and language of haole culture gradually absorbed the Japanese community.

In 1920 the federal survey commission reported: "Another handicap of serious character under which the public schools of the territory are laboring and with which there is nothing comparable in the states, is the system of foreign language schools which has grown to formidable proportions, particularly among the Japanese."

In the year in which the federal commissioners began their survey there were 163 Japanese language schools with an enrollment of 30,000 students and a teaching corps of 450, almost totally made up of teachers direct from Japan. In the face of this formidable foreign influence, the commission recommended the abolition of these schools. Fifteen years earlier there had been little concern over the development of the Japanese schools because it was thought that the majority of the Japanese would eventually return to Japan.

In 1922 the Territorial government passed an act designed to control and ultimately abolish the Japanese language schools. The act was contested vigorously by the Japanese community and in 1927 the United States Supreme Court ruled the act unconstitutional.

By 1930 a much more conciliatory attitude toward the language schools was evident. A subcommittee of Governor Judd's school survey commission reported

. . . The teaching of the language, history and philosophies of the great nations of Asia should be an important part of the common education in such a place as Hawaii. It is recommended that every reasonable and practicable effort be made to conserve in our educational process the values which lie in the languages, literature and cultures of Asia.

Although enlightened Islanders like Professor Romanzo Adams of the University of Hawaii understood that the language schools provided a vital link between the Oriental parent and child, an air of suspicion hung over the schools. This suspicion grew more or less intense depending upon relations between the United States and Japan.

On the eve of World War II the Japanese language schools enrolled more than 80 percent of all Japanese children. These were almost entirely children of first generation parents. In 1940 there were only 792 *Nisei* in the 45 to 64 age bracket, as against 21,717 *Issei*.[b] On the other hand, there were ninety-five thousand Nisei who were under 25 years of age, as against almost no Issei in that age bracket. Until the outbreak of the war the Issei were the dominant members of the Japanese community. The war would test the effects of the Japanese schools on the loyalty of the Nisei who had attended them, and would also see the rise of Nisei leadership in the Japanese community.

[b] The term *Issei* refers to first generation Japanese immigrants to the United States; they were ineligible for citizenship. *Nisei* refers to second generation American citizens of Issei parents.

Whereas the aims of the Japanese language school changed as greater and greater numbers of Japanese looked to Hawaii as their home, its clientele remained constant. In comparison, the aims of the English standard school remained constant while the composition of its clientele changed. For example, between 1925 and 1932, Oriental children at the Lincoln School, a standard school, never comprised more than 7 percent of the total enrollment. By 1939 this percentage had risen to 17. At Stevenson Junior High School 10 percent of the students were Oriental in 1929; in 1939 the percent had doubled and by 1943 one-third of the students were Oriental. This same rise in the proportion of Oriental students in the standard high school was evident.

A 1941 survey rated freshmen at the University of Hawaii according to oral English ability. From Roosevelt High School, the standard high school, 62 percent spoke standard English, 25 percent were found to have a slight variance from standard English, and 11 percent spoke with a marked dialect. Freshmen who came to the University from nonstandard high schools were judged as follows: 5 percent spoke standard English, 14 percent spoke with a slight variance, 25 percent spoke with a marked dialect, 41 percent had a "very marked" dialect, and 14 percent could not be understood by listeners who understood only standard English.

The standard schools had obviously protected the speech habits of those who spoke standard English as their first language and had provided a speech environment in which a minority of the nonhaoles could learn to use standard English. But the great bulk of nonhaoles completed their schooling without making intimate contact with standard English speakers, mainly the haole population.

The Effects of World War II on the Schools

The bombing of Pearl Harbor brought an instant halt to the Japanese language schools and other overt identification with Japanese culture. Martial law was declared only a few hours after the bombing as the Islands' people waited in terror of what the future might bring. Though the Islands' Japanese lived under a burden of suspicion and hostility, they gradually convinced even the most skeptical that, even though outward forms of American culture were not always evident, inwardly their loyalty was to America.

The war effort called upon Island children to rid themselves of all "foreign" characteristics and to be and speak "American." It brought thousands of standard-English-speakers into the Islands and sent thousands of Island men to mainland America and beyond, where they established closer contacts with haoles than they ever had in the Islands.

During the war 1,800 haole children were withdrawn from the English standard schools and evacuated to the mainland. There were 4,224 haole children in standard schools in the fall of 1941; by the end of 1942 there were only 1,261 left. This evacuation made room in the standard schools for many more nonhaole children than before, since the expansion of the standard schools had not kept pace with the increasing number of children who could meet the English requirement.

War conditions prevented the transportation of children beyond their own neighborhood school district lines as had been done in order to enroll children in standard schools. To preserve some of the old pattern, standard sections were added to nonstandard schools. At first there was resistance by standard school patrons, but the innovation was accepted and the practice spread quickly.

After 1945

On the basis of this wartime expedient, the territorial legislature mandated in 1945 that all non-standard schools open standard sections. The standard schools were allowed to operate as usual. Shortly thereafter the pressures to rid the Islands of their prewar class lines, the enthusiasm nonhaoles demonstrated in their new sense of power, and the improved quality of students' speech made possible a legislative plan to disestablish the standard school system. Beginning in 1949, and thereafter in all public schools, first graders would attend their neighborhood school. Those children in the second through twelfth grades would be allowed to continue in standard schools until graduation. Through this means the forces favoring standard schools were divided and the segregated system was gradually phased out.

As the segregated schools were phasing out, strong measures were taken by the Department of Public Instruction to bring the nonstandard schools up to the standards in oral English and academic achievement that had been required and developed in the standard schools. The legislature, now under the control of Democrats, became increasingly more liberal in financial support and more intimately involved with curricular affairs.

Patrons of the standard schools accepted the elimination of those schools partly on the grounds that all schools would become, in fact, English standard schools, meaning that "pidgin" would disappear and mainland achievement levels would be met. As would be expected, many standard school patrons, seeing the system being phased out, would not allow their children to become assimilated into a nonsegregated public school population, and sent their children to private schools instead. The usual argument was that the academic standards in the public schools were too low.

Given the differing functions ascribed historically to select or common schools or to standard or nonstandard schools, it is not unexpected that schools having an independent or quasi-independent status would be accepted as being schools of better quality. Inherent in this judgment was the assumption that schools catering to an essentially homogeneous clientele, culturally, linguistically, or intellectually, could provide students with a better education because of this homogeneity.

Whatever merit or lack of merit there was in that assumption, schooling in Hawaii from the missionary-inspired beginning onward did not proceed to assimilate the Islands' children by bringing the entire heterogeneous mixture together "eyeball to eyeball" in a common school, though an eye was kept open for the time when students emerging from schools were judged sufficiently alike to no longer justify segregation. This was the case with the disestablishment of the standard schools.

Why is it that an unusual number of private schools continue to exist in the Islands today? The private schools generally do not show a clear-cut pattern of cultural characteristics that they are trying to protect and perpetuate as was the case historically at Punahou, in the Japanese language schools, or in the English standard schools. Neither do they operate deliberately to bring together a wide diversity of students as was the case in the nineteenth century common schools or the nonstandard schools in the twentieth century.

The reasons for the continued existence of large numbers of private schools today are mostly linked to religion, economics, prestige, and tradition—plus, of course, a certain amount of propaganda. These are essentially intracultural rather than intercultural concerns and consequently have nothing at all to do with the question of whether or not they are American concerns. The Kamehameha Schools, however, represent a somewhat different case in some respects. There students are admitted on the basis of their Hawaiian ancestry. Not all children of Hawaiian ancestry can be accommodated and therefore further selection is made on the basis of ability and need.

This form of segregation is justified essentially on the grounds that the best interests of Hawaiian youth as well as of all Hawaii can be served this way. The Hawaiian youth and the Hawaiian community, it is believed, will better preserve their cultural and ethnic heritage and identity because of these schools. The schools, whose enrollment exceeds two thousand students, are in a real sense a memorial to the tragedy of Hawaiian culture and Hawaiian people. To some the schools exist in part to correct a gross imbalance between the cultural resources of the Hawaiians and other groups in the Islands; in a sense to protect and compensate Hawaiian youth for history's injustices. To others, the schools themselves are part of the tragedy because they continue to shelter the Hawaiians, refusing to help them learn to give and take with other Island youth.

Perhaps the Kamehameha Schools some day will be able to symbolize better than any other Island school the wider significance of Hawaii's remarkable experiment in assimilation, in which all ethnic groups share equally a respect for each other and profit equally from the benefits of their combined heritage.

Summary

We have seen in this study the implementation, according to the Islands' own unique setting and cultural circumstances, of characteristic patterns of development found wherever the transition has been made from traditional to industrial society. Assimilation of Hawaii's peoples came about within the context of the emergence of industrialism. With its technical evolutions and intellectual drive, industrialism aggressively transformed all aspects of the fundamental habits of thought and social behavior to fit American lines.

The Hawaiians, who had not moved very far from relatively simple patterns of living and working, and the Oriental peasant stock, to whom ideas of change and progress, science and technology were strange concepts and events, could not maintain their social apparatus and cultural characteristics that had developed prior to industrial civilization. Time softened the shock of eventual annihilation of most preindustrial cultural forms and schools supplied new forms to replace the old.

Industrialization required more technically and professionally trained people than the earlier privileged ranks could provide. Increasingly the need arose for industrialists to select personnel on performance rather than pedigree. Education had made people ready whenever such opportunities developed. New wealth and leisure, greater diversification of job opportunities, greater interdependence of the Islands' people, all were outcomes of industrialism and contributed toward making the Islands' peoples one people.

Hawaii's experience provides further evidence that psychosocial and linguistic evolution does not wait upon genetic evolution but is in fact Lamarckian in nature. Her history substantiates the fact that schools can be a real factor in the radical alteration of the inheritance transmitted from one generation to another. While protecting the cultural and linguistic heritage of the culturally advantaged haole, the schools also promoted the spread of those cultural and linguistic elements which gave all Islanders greater educational and social parity. Functioning both to meliorate and integrate conflicting forces and, at the same time, to maintain enough of the old cultural and linguistic heritage to give continuity between generations, the schools collectively played a central role in assimilating Hawaii's people into American culture.

3

Schooling for Minority Children

John E. Watson

The author is Director of the New Zealand Council for Educational Research. Like Ralph Stueber, in the preceding chapter, he is concerned with the school's contribution to social integration. He discusses the problems of providing adequate education for his country's distinctive minority, the Maoris. In a society which has attempted to provide equality, both social and educational, the attempt is not fully successful. It cannot succeed, Watson maintains, until more is known about three basic problems on which he focuses attention: language backgrounds, motivation for educational achievement, and conflicting values of home and school. He suggests that New Zealand's experience in dealing with such problems may help to clarify issues which are of significance and concern far beyond her borders.

The claim of individuals to be afforded an opportunity to achieve their full stature had become, at least in Western nations, a moral right conceded universally, and schooling is now regarded as one of the principal means through which a community can provide for that self-development. There is nothing especially new about this idea or its derivations, since proposals for equality in educational opportunity go back to the eighteenth century and beyond. But only in our time can it be said to have become one of the most dynamic of all the aspirations of people everywhere.

Much more recently men have begun to realize that an individual's ability to benefit from schooling is deeply influenced by his social location and experience. As a result of this additional understanding, a beginning has been made in recent decades to extend the basic moral principle to include opportunities for overcoming whatever obstacles stand in the way of self-development. Among more affluent nations which have already succeeded in providing at least ten years of schooling for all their young citizens, this newer concern has been expressed in the growing attention given to the quality of schooling available for those for whom such obstacles are conspicuous barriers, namely, the psychologically and physically incapacitated and the geographically and socially isolated.

Each of these extensions could be readily illustrated by developments which have taken place in New Zealand over the past quarter of a century or so. In a country of such strong equalitarian sentiment it is scarcely surprising that they should have been accepted there as natural and just extensions of other equalities already provided for. This does not mean, however, that they have been fulfilled in sufficient measure or even that their implications are invariably clear and well understood. Indeed, this paper had been stimulated by a widely felt need to sort out some of the critical questions that have begun to arise from efforts to expand the opportunities of the most recently recognized group of handicapped children, namely those who still reside in the sociological borderlands.

For the purposes of concrete illustration, the circumstances of Maori children in New Zealand will be used to provide the basic points of reference, since it is assumed that their situation is not unlike that of socially disadvantaged in many other parts of the world. The emphasis will be upon unresolved issues and uncertainties rather than the detail of accomplishment, administration, or organization; further, the questions examined will be those of daily concer to classroom teachers rather than those of interest to social scientists, administrators, or politicians. At this level many of the basic problems seem not to be bound by time or place; they afflict both large and small nations, the affluent as well as the poor, the old and the new. Those chosen for discussion are as follows:

1. The difficulties of teachers in understanding the needs of children who come to school with a language background which places them at a disadvantage in the normal context of classroom communication.
2. The difficulties of teachers in improving the motivation of children who come to school from situations which weaken their capacity for trust, self-confidence, and hope.
3. The difficulties faced by teachers who have to bear the brunt of transmitting the values of metropolitan enlightenment to communities or families caught up in the conflict of values associated with rapid social change.

There appear to be two main reasons why it may be profitable to examine the perplexities of a small, highly literate, relatively homogeneous nation in coping with problems of this kind. In the first place the issues that give concern in this, as in other fields in New Zealand, are now essentially those that affect the quality of schooling being provided. The complex quantitative problems of providing sufficient school places or teachers or services that still trouble larger or poorer nations have already been generally overcome. The issues to be clarified may be a foretaste, then, of difficulties that could emerge elsewhere when such logistical problems have been removed. Second, the setting in which these issues emerge has not been bedevilled by a history of deliberate segregation, separation, or ostracism. Varying degrees of social isolation aggravate the problems, it is true, but these are not the basis, or the direct result, of social policies. The Maori people are not inflamed by white exclusivism. If anything they are uneasy about inclusivist policies, for while they have adopted much of the culture of the *pakeha*,[a] they are not yet willing to have their Maori culture assimilated out of existence.

---

[a] When reference is made to relationships between Maori and European in New Zealand, the latter are also invariably called *pakehas* (pronounced "paakeha"). The word comes from the Maori word meaning foreigner, but it is now applied to all Europeans. The term "European" is less favored and the term "whites" is considered rather objectionable.

Essential Features of the Setting

To begin, it should be noted that like the minority groups of most nations, the Maori population is no more static or uniform than the dominant European population. Nor is it without traditions and deeply felt values. In brief, it is a mosaic of diverse history, tradition, and circumstance for which few generalizations can be offered without qualification.[1] Some Maori values affecting their contemporary educational and vocational aspirations could be traced back to their pre-European culture, even if they have been much buffeted and altered by two centuries of contact with Europeans. Others are a legacy of the disillusionment that followed from their encounter in the nineteenth century with the beginnings of European settlement. Defeated but by no means conquered, the Maori withdrew and in some areas held themselves apart from the Europeans for nearly half a century. Then gradually, as they turned into the twentieth century, their sense of identity was rekindled by the emergence of some notable and learned young leaders, the discovery of the nobility of the Maori past by European scholars, and by more benevolent governments.

The great public debate on the place of the Maori in the future of New Zealand, of which a reexamination of their schooling now forms only a part, is a result of their reentry in recent decades into extensive contact with the pakeha. This movement is a feature of the urban centers of the north [2] and has been promoted by a convergence of several factors: a gradual weakening of earlier grief and bitterness, paternalistic government policies, experiences in the armed forces, the lure of the cities for the younger generation, the effect of better schools, roads, mass media, their higher birth rate, shrinking land resources, and restricted opportunities for work and leisure in the hinterland. The story is a familiar one historically around the world and needs little emphasis.

As has also happened in other places and times, the abruptness of the migration of Maori youth to the cities has begun to create serious problems of vocational adjustment, which are already linked with visible evidence of social disorganization, discrimination, and inequality. The conscience of the present-day pakeha townsman is troubled by this evidence of disharmony, for he realizes that it does not settle happily with the equalitarianism that has long been a source of national pride. During more anxious moments he has also perceived that there are pockets of latent anti-Maori prejudice among the pakeha population which could become inflamed, and perhaps contagious, in less favorable times. Caught in a period of rapid economic growth and acute labor shortages, employers have also recognized that the Maori population contains an impressive reserve of talent and skill awaiting further development and deployment. It would be surprising if all this concern had not brought about a questioning of the assumptions under which Maori and pakeha have hitherto appeared to live in tranquility.

Such questioning, moreover, has been widespread, in town and country. It has been assisted by new scholarly publications, youth forums, wide coverage in the press and on radio and television, by new developments in the arts, new challenges on the sports fields, and new dimensions of foreign policy. It should be acknowledged at once that notable advances have already taken place in improving the health, education, employment, and material circumstances of the Maori people. Yet among both Maori and pakeha the conviction has gradually strengthened that the natural processes of social integration, social mobility, and accommodation will have to be greatly speeded up if the worst possibilities of the future are to be avoided.

The shaping of institutions to promote the mental and moral development of Maori youth is no new undertaking, of course. Quite arduous forms of institutional training for those fulfilling positions of leadership were in fact a feature of preliterate Maori society long before the arrival of the Europeans. Then, when the missionaries, following upon the whalers and traders, tried to introduce the Maori people to less demoralizing European ways early in the nineteenth century, many of them encountered an encouraging response, at least among certain strata of Maori society. Half a century or so later, legislative provisions were enacted to provide for the universal schooling of the Maori people, at a time when most other Western nations were laying the foundation of their school systems. In keeping with the wisdom of the times and the wishes of prominent Maori leaders, it was assumed that their welfare would best be attained by having them assimilate as speedily as possible the habits and usages of the European population. In good faith the community thus thought it was offering the Maori child full equality with the pakeha, and nearly a century passed before this basic premise was seriously questioned. Initially, the values of the schools to which Maori youngsters were sent had come from the other side of the world; the curriculum and the textbooks usually gave little heed to local needs, pakeha or Maori, let alone the traditions of the Maori people. This does not mean that leading administrators or teachers of the time were oblivious to things Maori, or to the complex issues of cultural contact, or that these policies were not welcomed by the Maori people. But the spirit of what was being offered is perhaps best symbolized by the fact that for a full century English has been the language of instruction encountered by Maori pupils at all levels of the school system.

Half a century had passed before educational authorities began to admit that these policies were failing. To perceptive administrators of the late 1920s it had become clear that much of what the Maori child was learning at school was not having much impact. Significantly, there never seems to have been any doubt that the Maori was as educable as the European, given the same opportunities—a reflection perhaps of the impact of their intellectual qualities upon the missionaries, and their astuteness in land negotiations and military strategy. From such reappraisals, however, a notable shift of emphasis occurred in the 1930s toward a more sensitive regard for their adaptive powers and their pride as a people. In the main this was expressed through a return to a "modified Maori curriculum" which attempted rather self-consciously to foster a wider appreciation of Maori history, arts, crafts, and song. At the same time provisions for scholarships, health and agricultural education, and the recruitment of Maoris into the teaching profession were all steadily expanded.

Through the past three decades, Maori school enrollments have increased fourfold. Like pakeha children, nearly all of them proceed automatically from elementary to secondary schooling and enjoy at least ten full years of schooling. All schools are open to all comers; Maori and pakeha sit in class together, and share equitably the basic equalities provided by legislation and regulation; teachers of comparable experience, age, and background; and similar equipment and facilities. Those differences that remain are not overtly determined on the basis of racial, economic, or political circumstances. Hence, while much still has to be done to improve the attendance and persistence of Maori pupils, relative to pakehas, the fundamental need is for a qualitative improvement of what is taught and how it is taught rather than a quantitative improvement in the number of school places.

The danger now is that abundant and misdirected goodwill advancing highminded reform could create a negative stereotype of Maori scholastic aspiration and achievement which would have serious consequences and become very difficult to eradicate. Already, it is claimed that such a stereotype is widespread among teachers. In many quarters it is of course realized that labels and stereotyped attitudes endanger the fluidity of relationships which have long been a feature of Maori-pakeha associations. Yet, despite the proliferation of reports and analyses, discerning assessments of the scholastic achievements of Maori pupils continue to be few, elusive, and rarely influential. The absence of carefully assembled information of this kind, and an anxiety about the community's reputation for racial tolerance, seem to increase the difficulties of teachers in understanding the nature of the inequalities being faced by their Maori pupils. In broad perspective, their vision is often blurred by a widespread inability to distinguish those features of the Maori child's situation that are the predictable outcomes, more or less, of either lower class status or social and geographical isolation, and those which are the residuals of his Maori heritage. It is the purpose of this paper to suggest that such a clarification would be pedagogically helpful as well as a wise and just precaution.

Speech and Thought

The main lines of the argument that follows can be illustrated very simply by the evidence available on the language development of Maori children, fragmentary though it is. Language and symbolic expression play a most important part in all aspects of school after all and, since they are the medium of a teacher's insight and skill, it is understandable that language difficulties should be seen by teachers as the most serious of the frustrations they face. Moreover, there is ample evidence to show that language accomplishments are particularly sensitive to the multiplicity of factors related to socially marginal or lower class children.

The one safe generalization that can be made about the language background of Maori children is that it is extraordinarily diverse. After nearly a century of being schooled relentlessly in the English language, it is a telling testimony that large proportions of Maori children are still able to respond to the Maori language, in some degree, in their homes or neighborhoods. From one field survey taking in many geographical areas and isolated districts as well as cities, it was estimated that a third of the Maori children were actively bilingual, and half were capable of understanding the Maori language in various degrees. Contrary to a common stereotype among non-Maori-speaking pakeha teachers, the author of this report asserts that the Maori being spoken by children brought up in a Maori-speaking environment is not generally of poor quality, and bilingualism does not appear to be a serious cause of difficulty with English.

The historical record leaves little doubt that the difficulties of teaching English to Maori pupils has been a subject of much concern to teachers since the latter part of the nineteenth century.[3] Furthermore, in broad outline, their definition of the problems has not changed much in that time. In the main, teachers can still agree only in general terms on the nature and frequency of their difficulties, and it is therefore not surprising that much uncertainty exists about the corrective actions required. When asked to list their difficulties, teachers of Maori children will commonly agree, with slightly differing emphases according to the level taught, that their main areas of concern are speech, comprehension, and written expression. Pressed to be specific about their difficulties, they will again agree that Maori children are handicapped by a limited vocabulary in English, because they use fewer adjectives, verbs, and qualifiers, because they prefer the present tense, the active voice, and personal pronouns, or because they omit connectives and confuse plural and singular forms. Again, it is common to find that these inadequacies are attributed to the cultural improverishment of the Maori home, to bilingual backgrounds, or to inadequate conceptual development.

Since this level of agreement seems to bear no relationship either to the degree of bilingualism of a given area or to the nature and incidence of errors showing up in tests and tape recordings, it is evident that these generalized opinions of teachers require closer scrutiny. In particular, the common assumption among many teachers and administrators that the home and mind of the Maori child are meagerly stocked and lacking in pattern seems especially worthy of closer attention. Precisely the same assumption by teachers of American Indians has been neatly described as part of a "vacuum ideology."[4]

It seems a rather significant coincidence that the generalized descriptions by teachers of the language difficulties that they encounter with Maori children parallel almost exactly the findings of a larger number of studies of the differences between the language of lower and middle class children in other countries. A decade ago Basil Bernstein,[5] of the University of London, summarized many of these studies to show that in general, and independent of verbal and non verbal IQ levels, the speech systems, linguistic codes, and written work of children brought up in working class homes are characterized by limitations in the vocabulary and the syntactical structures available to them.

With these facts Bernstein went on to develop a plausible theory of the relationships between social status, speech systems, modes of communication and perception which is no doubt attractive to many teachers. He postulated two codes of communication—the one a restricted code, always played out against a background of communal, self-consciously-held interests concerned with concrete needs and immediate consequences; the other an elaborate code of the middle class, characteristically involving more verbal planning which affects the lexicon, hesitation phenomena, and structural selection, and shows much more attention to accommodating the listener.

Numerous other analyses of language differences among social classes also seem agreed that the main differences lie at the level of syntactical organization. Although no studies of pakeha children are available in New Zealand to serve as checkpoints, it has already been concluded that Maori children "seem to be several years behind European children in their ability to control English syntactical structures adequately."[6]

The fact that teachers are perceiving their language difficulties with Maori children broadly in terms of the distinguishing features of the language of the lower class children of the great metropolitan centers of England and the U.S.A. raises some interesting questions. The Maori people, after all, are not yet a predominantly urban population. Could it be that the same language difficulties are not identified comparably for pakeha children from the laboring classes because they are located mainly in the cities and therefore not present in appreciable numbers where the Maori children are located? Is it that the social origins, training, and professional outlook of teachers make them especially sensitive to deviations from middle class speech patterns? Does the same background alert them to difficulties associated with social status but deflect them from those which originate from Maori patterns of thought and language?

In general, the statements of teachers suggest that they attach rather negative evaluations to the Maori language. Only a handful of teachers are able to converse in Maori, and the great majority do not have sufficient knowledge to act upon any appreciation that despite the variability in its use, the patterns of thought and verbal structuring associated with it are likely to persist long after it has fallen into disuse, if that should be its fate. As might be expected, the structure of the Maori language differs from English in important ways which, apart from phonemic and stress differences, also influence the choice of prepositions, verb patterns, and pronouns.

So far, very little has been done to identify what type of influence these differences have had upon the varying forms of English spoken by the Moari people. Indeed, it is doubtful whether the majority of teachers would be prepared to acknowledge the multidialectal nature of English as spoken in New Zealand, since they have a vested interest in the idea that only those who speak the prestige dialect speak correctly. Clearly, the variants of the English language that emerge in New Zealand in future years could be enriched by a conscious effort to accommodate the language heritages of its two main language traditions. But the point of this extended illustration is simply to draw attention to a specific gap in the knowledge of teachers which will be very hard to close if negative evaluations persist.

The obvious response is to suggest that the teachers who teach Maori children should be given some specialized training and equipped with suitable aids and manuals. Steps in these directions have already been taken, but the solution is not nearly so easy as it may at first appear. As with other children, the background circumstances of Maori children are endlessly variable; in addition, New Zealand has steadfastly resisted any administrative practices or forms of specialized training that could conceivably lock a group of teachers into some section or stratum of the teaching service. Moreover, as any teacher in the country may encounter Maori youngsters, it is theoretically difficult to justify mandatory basic training in Maori culture and language for a special group of teachers.

At the time when emphasis was on Europeanizing the Maori as quickly as possible, there was of course no issue of this kind about the type of training to be given to teachers of Maori children. It has become a question of some importance only with the contemporary ambition to accommodate and foster their cultural pride in a pluralistic society. The solution is not made easier by the fact that it is only in recent years that the secondary schools and universities have begun teaching Maori as a language for anyone who wishes to take it. Attractive textbooks and bulletins for teaching Maori as a language have appeared in greater numbers, but the reserve of knowledge of Maori among teachers is still meager. The shift of emphasis toward a greater appreciation of Maori culture, which began in the primary schools in the 1930s, did not reach the teachers' colleges and universities until the mid 1950s. And, as in the schools, it has mainly taken the form, so far as prospective teachers are concerned, of building up appreciative attitudes toward Maori history and art and toward Maoris as friends and colleagues. The point of the present analysis is to show that in terms of contemporary needs this is insufficient. Judged by teachers' difficulties in responding to the individual differences to be found among their Maori pupils, there now appears to be a clear need for additional training in diagnostic and remedial teaching related to language development.

The pattern of analysis used so sketchily here in analyzing teachers' perceptions of their difficulties in language work with Maori children could also be extended into several other areas of intellectual functioning. Viewed from the perplexities of teachers, there appears to be a clear case, for example, for a systematic examination of the etiology of skills of auditory discrimination among socially marginal children and, in the case of the Maori, some assessment of the relevance to schooling of their renowned oral traditions. Similarly, much clarification is needed of the difficulties that teachers associate with the inability of children, Maoris and others, to "think analytically and logically," and of their incapacities in regard to comprehension, imaginative thought, and intellectual adventuring. In passing we may note that the judgments of psychologists[7] on the basis of the minute samples of behavior tapped by Rorschach ink blot tests in socially fragmented rural communities, which have shown Maori youngsters to be lacking in originality, ultra-cautious, and deficient in imagination, could, if left at that, assume undue significance for teachers already committed to a vacuum ideology. At this level of debate it would not be difficult, however, to produce much more convincing and counterbalancing evidence of remarkable perceptive powers and imaginative insight that has been released by skillful teaching in communities equally improverished. [8]

Rather than polemics, what is required is a more penetrating pedagogical analysis of the specific intellectual skills that are insufficiently developed at particular ages, in particular communities or families, and of the specific pieces of experiential knowledge or appreciation that are missing or undernourished but essential. At the present time there is no clear evidence to show whether it is poverty and large families, or rural location and depressed social status, or Maori inheritance and patterns of child rearing, or some combination of all three of these conditions that is responsible for the type of intellectual functioning displayed by Maori children which teachers apparently consider restrictive, unhelpful, or countervailing.

Here again, if we were to speculate on the basis of what is known about the mental habits of lower class children of the great metropolitan centers of the Atlantic nations, we would wish to know whether the intellectual style of the rural Maori child is more physically and visually oriented than that of the more aural, verbally oriented child of the urban middle class; as well as whether they are more inductive than deductive, more externally oriented than introspective, more spatially oriented than temporal.

As we know, evidence has steadily accumulated to show that the generally inferior school achievement of children from the homes of manual workers is a reflection of pervasive differences in cognitive orientation and functioning operative from early childhood. [9] Children from homes of white collar workers, it has been shown, receive much more training in responding to the abstract, categorical, and relational properties of ideas and things, whereas children from the homes of manual workers tend to be trained to respond to concrete, tangible, immediate, and particularized properties. Such differences in approach bring about differences in perceptual dispositions that carry over into verbal expression, memory, concept formation, listening habits, and so on. It is almost inevitable, at present, that children from certain backgrounds will have difficulty understanding or following the cognitive style of their teacher.

This speculative analysis of relevant intellectual issues may have been sufficient to emphasize that the major difficulty in recommending programs that would be more precisely and promptly remedial is to decide upon the emphases that are appropriate for a given group of children. At present there are no soundly based pedagogical base lines from which to calculate the relevance of variations in their circumstances as they occur from one district to the next, in communities where kinship ties are strong compared with those of fragmented or migrant settlements, in multiracial compared with racially more homogeneous schools, for children from large families as compared with small families, or even between one Maori child and another.

For a given group of children, for example, it may be better to concentrate on training in auditory discrimination, memory skills, or anticipatory cues than on perceptual training or language skills. As in the case in lower class city children in other countries, it has been assumed in New Zealand that a concerted effort to improve the language skills of Maori pupils will have the most immediately pervasive effect in preparing them to profit from their schooling. This policy is more an expression of hope than a carefully substantiated prescription.

Response and Aspiration

Teachers everywhere encounter pupils who are timid, shy, and easily discouraged; one part of the art of teaching, indeed, is to draw out this inwardness to firmer ground. It is important, then, to keep a sense of perspective in considering a teacher's concern with the responsiveness of her pupils, for here we are near to the pulse of professional conscience.[10] Teachers of school beginners are usually more perceptive than most in recognizing that the introduction of a child to schooling requires tact, skill, and often delicacy. In the case of Maori children it would certainly be foolish to ignore the setting and the limitations of small country schools, or the happenstance presence of callow teachers. It would equally be foolhardy, however, to conclude that all Maori children are invariably unhappy or unresponsive or become so. Their preschool experience with adults seems likely to increase their need for a consistent and trusting relationship with a teacher. When it is offered they can be delightfully responsive. With these qualifications we turn to the concern of many teachers, administrators, and committees that a large proportion of the Maori youngsters seem unusually wary, or lacking in confidence, or uncommunicative, or embarrassed.

The timbre of these opinions differs somewhat, of course, according to the class level being taught: sensitive teachers of beginners are more concerned with the timid and bewildered; the elementary teachers with withdrawal or the fading out of early promise; secondary teachers with the diligence and persistence of the adolescent. All, in their various ways, are anxious to eliminate discords from the general harmony of their relationships with Maori pupils. Yet very few ever encounter vicious hostility, and the general school behavior of Maori pupils is no problem. The lacerating confrontations suffered by teachers coping with the slum children of some of the great metropolitan centers of the world are still almost unknown in New Zealand.

Some of the reasons for this diffidence and wariness are hardly exceptional or mysterious. In some isolated districts the Maori school entrant may know little more than a smattering of disconnected English words; links between the school and his home may be tenuous or nonexistent, and he may have never spoken to a pakeha before. His parents will almost certainly wish him to do well; they may have provided well for his health and happiness at home, but it is unlikely that they will know much about the practices of a modern classroom. Within the classroom, the children with the greatest command of English, usually pakehas or those from the more acculturated Maori homes, naturally make the best progress, while the fragile spirit of adventure among the others remains undernourished.

There are teachers who know these circumstances well, and many who have endeavored to cope with them with imagination and extraordinary patience.[11] For what is assumed to be a distressingly large proportion of Maori pupils, however, the frustration of not understanding, of not succeeding, of not being stimulated seems to become the seed bed for self-devaluations that subtly undermine a child's confidence to handle competently the challenge of competition with others. His basic insecurities gradually coalesce in a manner which sometimes parallels the Negro child[12] very closely. In fact the Maori child often seems aware of the unfavorable implications of racial membership even before he starts school. Such devaluations increase steadily in school and gradually switch from physical to intellectual or psychological criteria. Before primary schooling is over they have become important elements in the defensiveness of many Maori youngsters.[13]

The disharmonies implied here are not merely an outcome of inappropriate school objectives and organization or insufficiently sensitive teachers, however, even though each of these may aggravate basic features of the Maori temperament which condition their self-esteem. In a more fundamental sense the responsiveness of the Maori child reflects a personality pattern rooted in child-rearing practices, their cultural heritage, and contemporary circumstances. So far there have no systematic studies of the child-rearing practices of the dominant culture in New Zealand, but the "official" model of what is desirable is probably much closer to what Americans would recognize as the development pattern of middle class suburbia than to more exclusivist pressures of English middle class. This somewhat vague model is the point of reference in most discussions of child rearing in schools and churches, on radio and TV, in preschool centers and parents' manuals, and a discriminating measure of self-criticism toward it has not been formulated.[14] Hence the practices of Maori parents are usually judged, by inference, publicly and privately, in terms of middle class suburban ideology, with few charitable or insightful qualifications.

In point of fact, the only carefully developed psychological studies of child rearing in New Zealand are those that have been undertaken in Maori families. These have been conducted by a group of young psychologists stimulated by the late Ernest Beaglehole, whose distinguished record of research in the borderland between psychology and anthropology goes back over a quarter of a century. In the main, their observations were based on data collected in two rather dissimilar rural communities over the past two decades.[15] In order to "lay bare the social structure" of a "genotypical" community on the threshold of rapid change, these studies relied heavily upon projective measures of psychological states and processes, and deliberately avoided the customary analytical tools of social anthropologists.[16] The conceptual tools they have used for studying Maori personality, in its general modal form, are thus highly debatable. Still, they have offered many stimulating, well documented, and even ingenious speculations on personality development among the Maori from birth to adulthood.

In locating a fundamental benchmark, these scholars have attempted to separate out "the predominant motives . . . derivable from the developmental consequences of a salient childhood experience." Broadly and briefly, these include a high degree of independence on the part of the preschool child; participation in widespread but loosely organized and largely unsupervised play groups of prime importance as socializing agents and as a source of values and status; inconsistent and often sharp attempts at discipline by parents; a growing exposure to pakeha influences; increasing awareness of minority group status; fairly short-lived adolescent rebellion, followed by stern imposition of adult role behavior and standards. The consequences, so far as these authors interpret them, and in psychological genre, are deeply felt needs for responsiveness, expression, and conformity, and deep fears of failure, social isolation, emotional commitment, and out-group rejection.

The picture of Maori personality thus presented strikes directly at the root of the popular European conception of Maoris as warm, friendly, happy-go-lucky, and uncomplicated persons. Not surprisingly, these authors consider this to be a grossly superficial stereotype testifying mainly to the indifference of pakehas to the real state of mind and values of the Maori. If the detail of Maori child rearing is examined in terms of Erickson's eight sequential phases of identity formation,[17] it is clear, Ritchie asserts, that the disruptions of the Maori child's expectations of trust, reciprocity, fidelity, and generosity begin to occur very soon after he leaves the warm, indulgent atmosphere of infancy.

As a result, we are told, he retains sufficient hope for optimism, but is unable to develop much trust in having his expectations fulfilled. Committed early to developing identity in sibling and peer groups rather than the family, he soon becomes habituated to fending for himself, to resolving the conflicts of the child world by denial and avoidance, to bottling up his grievances and not expecting much sympathy from adults, to being especially sensitive to judgments of his peers but wary of deep and lasting friendships with them.

The deeper sources of his conflicts are the community's expectations that he will value his Maori identity, while he is continuously being made to feel ashamed of it. Unless he competes successfully in the world defined by the pakeha, he is "letting his race down"; if he withdraws from the pakeha world, and becomes more Maori, he lets his parents down. Thus personal worth becomes judged by group membership regardless of individual merit. Shame sanctions figure prominently in the disciplinary measures used by Maori parents; they also have magnetic attraction in psychological explanations.

The result of these inconsistencies and uncertainties is that the Maori child and youth is often immobilized by *whakama* (a Maori term meaning embarrassment, shyness, and alienation) whenever he finds himself outside the range of ordinary events. These feelings may be so intense that he can rarely communicate much of what he feels, let alone the reasons for it, and his capacity for achievement and free mingling is immediately stultified. Indeed, so much so that, in Ritchie's view, "whakama is a more significant potential difficulty than pakeha prejudice" in providing for Maori fulfilment and much "less easy to eliminate or reduce."

As stated, it originates, in psychological terms, in the inconsistencies inherent in the development of a divided identity. While the pakeha world must bear some of the blame for this failure in the confidence of the Maori child, the more serious and immediate inadequacies seem to emerge from the difficulties of Maori parents in identifying themselves with the aspirations of young persons growing up in a rapidly changing environment. Reticence over such issues as story telling, homework, advice on schooling and vocations, and so on, may be interpreted therefore not simply as issues of time or neglect but as surface manifestations of much deeper conflicts that are not uncommon among groups standing marginally between a fading past and an unachieved future.

In the lives of most individuals such conflicts are accentuated at the point where decisions must be made about the relevance of schooling to vocational prospects and life chances. Like so many young people of our time, young Maoris are today obliged to become a new race of men hewing out a fresh identity without satisfactory models or sure patterns. Even the most sympathetic of their teachers and counselors may appear to be less helpful than their parents in offering guidance. Assumptions that this or that Maori pupil is simply a "brown-skinned pakeha" are easily made, and quickly limit the acceptability of the advice given.

In contrast to the pattern of middle class suburbia, the Maori adult community seems to be rather more actively concerned with the behavior of adolescents than it is with childhood and it imposes more pressure on them to conform. In addition, the period of marginality and rebellion for Maori youth is usually shorter, less preparatory, and less exasperating than it is for middle class European youth. Instead of being a period of emancipation, the teen years of young Maoris are often a period of rapprochement with home and family, a phase when emotional ties with parents are strengthened. Within a relatively short period of a year or two, a Maori adolescent acquires a status among his own people of a junior adult and, especially in the case of the male, immediately enjoys the privileges of the unmarried. With brilliantine, gay clothes, good wages, and relative freedom from family and community commitments, he does not take long to regain his poise and sociability, at least outwardly. Schooling must often seem a dull and irrelevant alternative.

Taking account of these circumstances, and their association with rural location, scholastic handicaps, and the material benefits to be gained by early employment, it might be anticipated that Maori youth would differ appreciably from other secondary school youth in both their educational and vocational aspirations, as well as their motivation to achieve them. The only really systematic attempt to clarify the nature of these differences was undertaken several years ago by David Ausubel.[18] He chose rural and urban samples, and then endeavored to match them with pakeha control groups. Then, by means of interviews, observation, and questionnaires, he sought to identify the cultural uniformities and differences in the aspirations of each group, their prestige needs, achievement imagery, and so on. With populations so different demographically it was not easy to adopt this design in a meaningful way. Nevertheless, within the limits of localities studied and the instruments used, this study does confirm that the hopes, motives, felt pressures, and degrees of naiveté of Maori and pakeha youngsters from working class homes are much more alike than they are different.

Ausubel considered this to be a finding of tremendous psychological and cultural significance, since it seemed to confirm that acculturation "has proceeded to the point where it can sustain the generation . . . if not the implementation . . . of European educational and occupational ambitions." Their ambitions reflect, of course, the prevailing achievement ideology to which they are exposed in schools, in guidance programs, and in the wider culture, as well as the publicly expressed desires of their parents.

Ausubel goes on to claim, however, that privately the latter were more oriented toward Maori criteria of success, and since they have no deep commitment to pakeha achievement values, they do not consistently encourage their implementation. For the early years of adolescence, school and the wider culture seem to predominate in setting up the hopes of youth. Later, as communication improves with parents and the Maori adult community, the values and tensions of Maori life become more influential. For a large proportion, school-based motivations have not been absorbed with sufficient conviction or depth to persist in the absence of consistent encouragement, or to cope with teenage sensitivity toward slights and discrimination, real or unintentional.

In situation and attitude, the plight of Maori parents today has many parallels with that of pakeha parents of a generation ago. The levels of schooling they achieved themselves mean that it is now unreasonable to expect them to be precisely informed on the relevance of academic achievement to vocational success in contemporary circumstances. With larger families and smaller incomes, there are also limits on the extent which they can enter into commitments involving long term vocational preparation for their sons and daughters.

Yet despite all these handicaps—assumed, speculative, or real—no convincing evidence has been produced to show that Maori youth are any less upwardly mobile, or less willing or less able to enter middle class occupations, than their pakeha age mates from similar backgrounds. Where a Maori family is well anchored in a kin-based community, we assume it does not teach very explicitly that moving up the European social scale is an especially desirable and virtuous activity. But in more fragmented communities, or in the city, where increasing numbers have migrated, the situation is by no means clear.

Much effort, many exhortations, and numerous and interesting programs for scholarship support and better vocational guidance or placement in New

Zealand are based on the assumption that longer schooling and comparable academic success between Maori and pakeha is an indispensable precondition for social harmony. Once again, this is a very plausible hypothesis, much welcomed by administrators and possibly sufficient as a basis for short term amelioration. But it remains a hypothesis all the same. When exalted to a principle, it seems to encourage short term solutions that deflect attention away from the more fundamental responsibility of teachers for freeing the human intellect. Whatever his job or income, fulfillment for the Maori, as for others, depends upon his capacity and freedom to imagine, to enjoy, to choose and modify the culture in which he finds himself. What kinds of teachers and schooling best promote these capacities?

Uniting School and Community

At base, the gravest problems affecting the schooling of the Maori are those associated with the articulation of the contrasting value systems of school and home. Deep within many Maori hearts resentment for past wrongs and indifference continues to smoulder, irk, and sometimes overwhelm; the base of corporate solidarity for many has been shattered; whatever the source of their new self-respect, it has still to find validation. Only a fortunate few have already found it in their religion.

Universally, however, the public school is the dominant agency and daily reminder of change—irreversible change—change that many fear will bring about the ultimate dissolution of what remains of the core of their corporate identity. Each day as their children go forth to school, parents and grand-parents are reminded that the values of that core which the older generation still finds worthy are acting to the detriment of the new generation. Thus a breach between the generations is opened. And while their children remain in the shadow, this painful process of adjustment strikes directly at the nerve center of parental control, which is always based on the special wisdom of adults.

Despite much profession of good will, encouragement of the arts of Maori life, and a growing recognition of the place of language in cultural pride, it is still apparent that the public schools of New Zealand have not yet generally taken into account, in any positive sense, the resilience and continuing relevance of Maori values. There have been countless teachers, it is true, who have labored in Maori communities with tact and wisdom, and who have been richly rewarded by the affection extended to them. Such mediators are comparatively rare, it seems, a special breed perhaps, and their power has been almost always localized, transient, and conditional.[19]

More commonly, large numbers of teachers become distressed by what they interpret to be apathy, neglect, depravity, instability, and cultural poverty within the Maori home.[20] For young men and women nostalgic for the pleasures of city and suburb, or overanxious about professional advancement, these frustrations are especially telling. It would certainly be foolish to ignore the existence of poverty and demoralization, but the much more impressive need is to recognize the nature of the deep concern for education presently in evidence among the vast majority of Maori parents.

Once again, the historical record suggests that generally speaking, Maori parents (and grandparents) have always been concerned about the schooling being received by their children. Schools and their staffs and activities, a number of community studies confirm,[21] are among the most prominent topics of daily discussion, debate, and criticism. The intensity of this interest is significant, considering the inadequacies of the means for giving expression to it and the limitations of the links that inform it. Such family or neighborhood discussions do not appear to be directed negatively at teachers on the whole, but they are much preoccupied with the potent and potentially beneficial role of the school. It is unfortunate then that, when known, they appear to put many teachers on the defensive. Alternatively, assumed silence is too often misinterpreted, particularly among young, inexperienced, or the especially earnest teachers, as a sign of either ingratitude or benevolent compliance. The striking social (and possibly intellectual) distances which exist between teachers and parents ensure that such private assessments are not often unsettled by public exposure. More than 30 years ago, Willard Waller invoked Simmel's concept of "the stranger" to provide a brilliant analysis of a teacher's plight in situations like this.[22]

Quite clearly these breakdowns in communication are more an outcome of divergent values, social distance, and incompatible roles than of school organization, although the transient nature of school staffing in many country districts seems likely to aggravate this situation. The tragedy is twofold: first, for teachers—even Maori teachers—it is by no means easy to accommodate the reinforcing elements in the conception of the tasks of the teacher that is held by Maori parents; second, the respect for and appreciation of the school shown by Maori parents remains highly generalized and ambivalent. Their affirmative expectations, often influenced by a knowledge of the superior standards set by leading city or boarding schools, are not particularized in a way that enables them to contribute positively to the fulfillment of those objectives of their local school which are of deep relevance to them. In short, within the confines of their immediate community, the Maori people do not yet share fully in owning the schools attended by their children. The more closely knit the community, it seems, the more complete this isolation.

Ultimately, the source of these discontinuities lies in the locus of power which determines the philosophy governing the schools. For more than a century in New Zealand the emphasis has been upon what the school, or a benevolent government, brings to the Maori child, rather than on what the Maori child brings to his school. In comparative terms, the New Zealand school system has done well in removing the inequalities of wealth and geography, in ensuring that the Maori child is not discriminated against in terms of the facilities, teachers, scholarships, and services available to him. Indeed, in some ways he may enjoy preferential treatment, and the mood of the nation is to make this more so. Further, much progress has been made in removing inequalities that originate in intellectual potential and emotional well-being. In fact, there is a tendency to define the problems of Maori schooling as "just part of the larger problem of recognizing individual differences in their depth and complexity."[23]

But sufficient progress cannot yet be claimed in recognizing the new dimension of inequality that now worries schoolmen wrestling with the problem of providing for human fulfillment in environments as different as the slums of New York or the villages of Asia. This is the realization that no school system can claim to be just which is organized in such a way as to favor children who have been socialized in one rather than another part of the social structure of the community that nourishes them. Wherever a school system is simply an extension of the homes of an urban middle class, or of a dominant culture, or both, it is inevitable that the children from those homes will be in the best position to profit from it.

In pakeha terms, the middle class component of the Maori population is still very small, and unlikely to expand rapidly. Hence, until the schools of New Zealand are able to accommodate with more skill and discrimination the relationships and tenor of the present social structure that nurtures the Maori child—until they can resolve the conflict of roles in which he is often now involved, and offer accomplishments that have real meaning for him in his search for valid identity—the legitimation of educational change for the Maori people will subsist on the quicksands of expediency.

Still, the situation is not without promise. Already major shifts have begun to occur at the national, regional, and community level in a realignment of the agencies responsible for administering schools attended by Maori pupils, and in the opportunities available to the Maori people to influence the direction of change and to participate in the tasks of the schools. Fresh proposals from the Maori people for improved materials and more skillful teaching of their language and heritage have been welcomed, and acted upon.

As a result, the Maori people have begun to respond with some vigor and enthusiasm to the invitation to help shape national objectives. In increasing numbers they are being elected to school committees, parent-teacher associations, the controlling authorities of preschool and secondary school services, as well as numerous other public offices from the local to the national level. The all-important redistribution of power is therefore underway, at least in organizational terms.

As is to be expected, the most critical areas for its expression continue to be the community relationships of individual schools and teachers. Moreover, up to a point, the basic situation applies to schools everywhere and not simply to schools enrolling Maori pupils. It is an interesting feature of the centrally financed New Zealand school system that parent-teacher cooperation is extensive at the local level, on international standards, and that teachers generally seem less anxious about these relationships than elsewhere. This does not mean that the fundamental tensions of the relationship have been removed; viewed sociologically, parental participation remains selective numerically, occupationally, and on issues communicated, just as it does in systems with a higher degree of local financing. Nevertheless, the broad features of the situation apply to Maori parents as much as pakehas.

But in the case of Maori parents there are, in addition, more subtle and deeper issues which are best viewed through sociological binoculars. Since the schools Maoris attend are located in widely varying communities, there are some hazards in generalization, but to the extent that they are still basically a rural people the more usual situations tend to cluster toward the folk end of what some sociologists have been pleased to call the sacred-secular continuum.[24]

Redfield and Toynbee[25] have already noted that the more naturalistic concepts, such as the folk society and so on, are not easy to apply to contemporary Maori communities. Yet in most of them, local tribal history and its consequences in attitudes and feelings, different evaluations of material property and human destiny, and different modes of social relationships still constitute a social reality, more or less integrated, that differs sharply from that of the pakeha in town or country. There are limitations in using the concept of sacred-secular continuum to handle these differences in an integrative manner, but it will serve for the purposes of illustration.

Viewed at the extreme, a distinguishing feature of the public school teacher's life in the "sacred" community is its restriction to his classroom role. He is given little option but to remain socially unattached and psychologically detached, whatever his private feelings are about the community. The community almost deliberately limits him to this role so that it can preserve the folk values at the core of its homogeneity, and in order to preserve the status quo of its own social structure and organization.

Every teacher, but especially the one who is a representative of a dominant or secular or urban order, becomes an imminent and every-present threat to the very heart of such a community because his purpose is to detach and set free the bearers of its heritage. Coming from the outside, he is a carrier of new ideas and new conceptions of action (future oriented and problem centered), and with them he touches the community on its most tender spot, its children. His pupils cannot help but carry the local culture into the schools with them, and if its values and standards of conduct are to survive, they must continue to hold it in their possession. As it happens, a child's attitudes will follow those of his elders, so that if they are ambivalent, he is likely to become so. He alternatively admires and rejects the school, and thus the teacher becomes the subject of mixed feelings by both children and adults.

This sort of situation is not as unusual as many New Zealanders would like to believe, and it has significant implications for the teacher. Whether he wills it or not, the teacher's impact tends to be restricted to the narrow band of discretion available to him within the secular functions of the classroom or other secular functions in the community, help with form filling, and so on. Any transgressions from this definition of his role are carefully watched, gossiped about, and usually countered rather subtly. His position, it is important to note, is defined by structural features of the situation, not by private feelings; only a few exceptional teachers (often married teaching couples in New Zealand) manage to establish some bridges across these structural barriers that are capable of carrying limited and carefully defined traffic. Naturally the situation changes according to the location of a particular community along this continuum, and at the secular (usually urban) end, where increasing proportions of Maoris are moving, it is probably defined more by social class than by cultural variables.

The broad structural features of this type of analysis constitute a long and distinguished heritage in the literature of sociology and social anthropology. Unfortunately, it does not seem to have often been used to study school-community relationships and our knowledge of these matters seems too simple to be helpful. As elsewhere, it is widely professed in New Zealand that good teaching requires teachers who know fully the social and cultural circumstances in which their pupils are placed, as well as the resources of the community.

Indeed, the very enlightened regulations laid down for the guidance of teachers in Maori village schools in 1880 stated quite specifically that teachers should not confine themselves to mere "school instruction," and over the years countless numbers of teachers have adopted this advice with exemplary dedication. But within the instructional role it is generally acknowledged that a teacher's transient or marginal status in a community militates against his classroom competence. Without intimate associations with the community, it is asserted, teachers are inadequately placed to integrate into the school's scholastic and corporate life questions that are of vital and immediate concern to their pupils.

It so happens that the New Zealand situation presents an almost unrivalled opportunity to test the validity of these assumptions. For over 30 years, for instance, a deliberate attempt has been made to foster Maori history, arts, and crafts in schools attended by Maori children, and now more generally. There is little doubt that this relatively minor modification of the urban oriented curriculum has considerable value in reducing a little the social distance between teacher and pupils, in increasing parental appreciation, in providing a sort of spasmodic emotional bonding for Maori pupils in particular, and in offering an area of limited success for them.

Yet such additions are not always welcomed by Maori pupils (whatever the feelings of their parents), and they often appear to remain an enclave in the curriculum, apart from also being poorly taught on occasions (and perhaps generally). Such lessons do not seem to be often informed by what may be of cosmic interest in local tribal history and its consequences in attitudes, or feelings, or questions of concern to the local people and their children. Here too is yet another example of an innovation based upon hope and obvious charity, possibly very beneficial, but extremely difficult to evaluate. No pedagogically significant points of measurement have been established.

Neither in New Zealand nor anywhere else does there appear to have been any systematic, carefully disciplined effort to test whether a teacher's knowledge of the local scene, or his participation in it, has any significant effect upon his interest or capacity to integrate this knowledge into the scholastic work of his classroom, or into the emotional toning of his relationships with pupils. This is not only an issue affecting the fulfillment of children; quite plainly, the restrictiveness of the teacher's role, both socially and intellectually, is a matter of some moment, since it is also a major source of his basic pedagogical frustrations.

The teacher carries with him one kind of key that may unlock some of the deepest aspirations of those who come to him. If he fumbles with it in anger or despair, the whole purpose of his mission is undermined. We should acknowledge that there are no static solutions to dilemmas of this kind. They are the inevitable concomitant of the effort to inject secular values into a sacred community, and as the advance guard of that invasion, teachers have to be prepared to bear the brunt of the conflict that follows. Such a confrontation between the forces desirous of change and those resistant to change is inevitable in the exercise of power. On both sides there is still scope for improving tactics and strategy.

Conclusion

The issues dealt with in this paper are neither unique nor exceptional. Indeed, the problems of improving the schooling of Maori children have been explored for the purpose of developing a minute snapshot of a limited range of themes in a drama now being played on a worldwide stage. Snapshots usually have the disadvantage of being static, selective, and quickly forgotten. The one shown here has been taken in a small country that has little power to influence the councils of the world. Although enjoying a relatively high standard of material comfort, it is not a wealthy country (as is often assumed) and its capacity to assist less fortunate people with financial aid or personnel is strictly limited. Yet its smallness, remoteness, literateness, and standard of comfort could, given sufficient wit and humility, make it a very promising field station in which to clarify pedagogical issues of universal significance. The outcome of the present courtship between Polynesia and Europe may yet provide the distinctiveness of New Zealand's own contribution to that clarification.

4

Educational Aspirations as a New Social Force

Cole S. Brembeck

Perhaps the most frequently mentioned feature of education in the modern era is the dramatically growing desire for education in developing countries. The author reports a study made by interviewing parents, teachers, and other educational personnel in three Asian countries. He presents his findings in relation to six hypotheses concerning the "social and psychological consequences of the influx into schools of many students who for the most part come from unschooled traditions."

One of the pervasive facts about formal education in the developing countries is simply that more people want it. More parents than ever before want their children to go to school, more children are actually going, and they are staying in school longer. Few enterprises in the developing world can match education in its growing popularity and appeal.

The desire to go to school is reaching out to new segments of the population previously untouched by formal education, from urbanites in the great cities to villagers and peasants in the fertile plains and valleys, and on to tribesmen in the remote hills beyond. This rising demand for education, frequently amidst poverty, is symbolized in the remarks of a Pakistani village patriarch, when he was asked how it was that when in his village there was no light bulb, no running water save a dirty stream, no wheel, the villagers were willing to dig into their own pockets to build a school for their children. "Sir," he said with great dignity, his white beard glistening in the evening sun, "we want our children to have something better. How can they unless they get an education?"

The quantitative explosion in the demand for education presses upon educational planners the need to attend to certain matters, frequently to the exclusion of others. Items which absorb the energies are those which are obviously in short supply. There is not enough money, enough teachers, enough school buildings, and enough books. There are usually more than enough students. Educational planning thus becomes an exercise, and a crucial one, of developing strategies for getting maximum educational returns on meager educational investments.

Critical though this exercise is, it diverts attention from another vital aspect of the new quantity dimension in education: What is happening to the schools? What is the influx of new students, taught by new teachers in new schools, set in communities frequently new to formal education, doing to the education process? In short, how are rising educational aspirations influencing the social conditions under which students learn and teachers teach?

What happens to those who aspire to move up by means of education is a matter of deep concern in both developing and developed countries. The development of human talent is now being viewed in a new light. On the one hand, there is an awakening humanistic concern for those of humble origin who seek to improve themselves. On the other, there is the element of national self-interest in the full utilization of human resources. Their conservation and enhancement is of primary concern in all nations regardless of their stage of development.

This study looks at but one aspect of this broad subject, namely some of the social and psychological consequences of the influx into the schools of many students who for the most part come from unschooled traditions, frequently the first of their families to enter a classroom, and who seem determined to gain admission to the cosmopolitan world of the educated.

To learn more about some of the social determinants influencing school learning within the context of rising aspirations, I decided to interview people in India, Pakistan, and the Philippines who were close to this development and who were in a position to be knowledgeable about it. There was no attempt to conduct a controlled study, nor to quantify the results.

One hundred and twenty-five people were interviewed. They included parents, teachers, headmasters, school inspectors, and other middle level administrative personnel; high level education leaders; and a few Americans assigned to overseas education missions of various types. The average interview took two and one-half hours, with a range of from one to four. In a number of instances the interviewee graciously permitted me to return a second time, and in several instances a third, in order to follow up on productive lines. What is reported in this paper is limited to the content of the interviews and my perception of it.

Assumptions

I began with certain assumptions which should be exposed to view.

1. Rising educational aspirations in the developing countries constitute a new social force having little-understood but far-reaching influences on the education process.
2. The introduction into the schools of vast numbers of new students alters existing conditions of learning, and adds new ones not previously present.
3. A significant segment of the new student population comes from families and social class backgrounds uninitiated in the values of formal education.
4. Modifications in the conditions of school learning are in the direction of accommodating dissimilar value systems and the resolution of tensions arising from their confrontation.
5. A framework for understanding the conditions of learning in the developing setting is to be found in the concept of cross-cultural education, in which educators of one cultural tradition confront students and parents of another.
6. Rising educational aspirations and their resulting impact upon the con-

ditions of school learning take place within the larger context of social change and are meaningful only as they are linked to the content of social change.

Hypotheses

Taking these assumptions, I constructed six hypotheses in order to give focus to lines of inquiry and to provide check points against which interview returns could be compared.

1. The first hypothesis is that rising demands for education, coupled with actual higher levels of educational achievement, result in challenges to the existing control of education and may lead to shifts in the locus of power. This hypothesis affirms that there is a positive relationship between the amount of educational opportunity provided and the breadth of interest in, if not actual legal participation in, its control. As educational opportunity spreads out and down the socioeconomic structure, so will the interest in the nature of education and its control. If this hypothesis is affirmed, we would expect that one of its manifestations will be a growing situation of uneasy tension, and possibly contention, between the controllers and consumers of education.

2. As education is extended to the masses, the goals of the school will shift in two directions: (a) from teaching purely intellectual skills to the full socialization of the child through his adolescence, and (b) the assimilation of children of "deviant" ethnic and social backgrounds into the dominant culture. This hypothesis suggests that rising educational aspirations bear a direct relationship to the functions of the school and may result in shifts in educational goals and practices from narrow intellectual ends to broad social purposes. It is further hypothesized that this shift in goals will be accompanied by social conflict about the proper goals of education and their determination.

3. Shifts toward the socialization of the whole child and his assimilation into the dominant culture accentuate the rise in the school of an adolescent society whose values are neither those of the education establishment nor those of the families from which the students come. It is hypothesized that this development of an adolescent society within the schools results from a combination of several circumstances: (a) the child is moved to the school from a traditional family which was formerly responsible for his total socialization; (b) the linkage between the family and the school is weak, providing for the child no real bridge by which to make the transition, leaving him largely to find direction in his peer group; and (c) the teacher and others in the school hold values which are at variance with those of the home. The school thus provides

for youths who are removed from traditional homes, and are strangers to the new values which the school represents, an ideal environment to develop their collective resources as age mates. With weakening allegiance to the family and its social control, with awakening interest in metropolitan values of a school which does not at the same time provide effective control, youths experience a new freedom unknown to their parents.

4. The more the school encompasses the child, the greater will be its impact as a social institution. This hypothesis assumes that the schools of emerging nations are moving through a cycle, as social institutions, from narrow, restricted purposes and influence with a few students to the broad preemption of the time and energies of many students; and that the growth of the school as a social institution enlarges in direct proportion to the life energies of children consumed.

5. Increasing demand for education from nonelite groups encounters opposition from the elite who control education. This pressure from beneath provides elite groups with a rationale for maintaining present, and establishing new, educational programs designed to perpetuate their preferred status. The social class purpose of such elite programs is to counter and control the extension of mass education.

It is further hypothesized that this reaction will find its legitimation among the elite in arguments which mask the social class struggle involved in the movement from selective to mass education, and that such arguments will be expressed in the concern for maintaining high standards of education regardless of cost, for being highly selective in admission policies, for limiting educational opportunities to proven manpower needs, and for providing a range of low status educational opportunities (mostly in vocational areas) for the purpose of diverting the student stream from higher levels of education, status, and power.

6. Increasing demands for education accentuate the cultural discontinuity between home and school. To children reared in traditional village environments the atmosphere of the school may be quite incomprehensible. With the child's growing awareness of social reality, he finds himself spending many of his waking hours in a school in which his elder kin, and source of authority, are mentally and physically absent. Meanwhile, he confronts a teacher who has difficulty understanding the values of the parent villagers, who embraces metropolitan values, and who may regard his students as belonging to an inferior culture.

If the parent and teacher maintain some degree of meaningful contact, this incipient discontinuity between home and school may be meliorated. But when the teacher feels that his main responsibility is to an educational bureaucracy in a distant city, rather than to the local community, the school room may be a focal point for feelings of tension and alienation.

The Sources of Educational Aspirations

To what do people attribute their rising desire for schooling? The wellsprings of motivation which cause people to lift their educational aspirations are undoubtedly complex and screened from the interviewer's probing look. The explicit reasons which people give provide but a glimpse of those which are implicit. The interview data does, however, permit us to isolate a few of the factors which people think are influential in their desire to be educated, as well as some of those which counter the trend toward additional schooling.

Educational aspirations are nurtured within a social context. The varieties of social contexts, however, which are capable of stimulating educational ambition are infinite. American studies which give considerable weight to the influence of social class in the determination of educational aspiration did not prepare me fully for what respondents said repeatedly in the interviews. That educational aspiration is stimulated by the vast multiple reinforcements associated with social class position seems quite clear. But how does one explain high educational aspiration when it is found almost in isolation, cut off from the usual reinforcements which we associate with the desire to be educated: family educational traditions, peer group approval, high levels of community educational achievement, free schools, and status motivations?

In the absence of these, one looks for other less obvious but singularly strong determinants of educational aspiration. One also begins to suspect that these determinants are less respectful of social class lines than we sometimes think, that select, strong, motivating forces, operating atypically within the social context, can result in a kind of tenacious desire for schooling not found in the rich and congenial atmosphere of the well educated middle classes. Can it be that the very factors which we associate with social disadvantage in a developed country may, within the context of a developing one, spur rather than deter educational aspiration?

The evidence gathered in these interviews would suggest the possibility that the large numbers of students now overflowing the schools of developing nations come from socioeconomic settings associated in western countries with low, rather than high, educational aspiration. Indeed, it suggests the value of raising this question: Could it be that when social disadvantage is of a certain character and composed of certain ingredients it may create a milieu peculiarly capable of spurring educational aspiration by the very force of its negative persuasion?

Credence to the question is given by the large number of respondents who indicated that they came from families where the parents were illiterate, where the village looked upon them with suspicion when they went to school, where alienation from the group was part of the price of schooling, and where schooling generated a high level of personal conflict and frustration. What these peculiar ingredients might be can only be hinted at from the responses in the interviews. Most of the respondents who achieved levels of education higher than their social environments would normally suggest did, however, point to some clues, which we now consider briefly.

Most of these respondents were influenced by a parent, sometimes the father, but frequently the mother. In a number of instances the mother was illiterate, or she possessed very meager schooling. Yet, it was this unschooled person who instilled in the child, most frequently the son, the desire to go to school:

My mother could neither read nor write and she knew few people who did. One day she called me to her and said, "You are going to secondary school in the city. You will be the first from our village to go." I said that I would feel strange working in the fields with the others when they learned I was going to get a Western education. "They will poke fun at me and say I am too good for them." She said, "That is all right. I will explain to them." So it was that I got an education. She would be pleased to see me in this seat now.

In the joint family it is sometimes an uncle who provides the motivation to be educated. Not finding educational encouragement in the parents, the child may find it in another person of the kin group with whom he is likely to have close and continuing contact as he grows up:

I attribute much of my interest in education to the nature of the joint family in which I grew up. In our family there were two uncles for whom I had a great deal of regard, and they urged me to get an education, to work hard, and to get ahead. In our family there were many adult models and a child could adopt any one of them. If one did not suit him, he could choose another. We were a poor family but my two uncles encouraged me to get an education anyway.

A person who can serve as an educated model is usually available to the parent or child or both. The model may be found within the family or it may be a teacher or a government officer who has come to the village speaking excellent English, wearing fine clothes, and looking prosperous:

Please write this down. We are brothers from Hunza State, high in the mountains. Legend says that we are decendents of Alexander the Great, who brought his army into Hunza when he marched into India. You notice that we have blue eyes and Greek noses.

We are the first ones to come out of Hunza State to be educated at the University because our father was ambitious for us to get an education. That was our father's highest ambition for us: "I can't go, but I want my sons to go," he said. Our father learned about education from seeing British officers of the Gilgit Agency and he wanted his sons to be like these officers, who wore good clothes, spoke well, and lived in good houses. Our father learned about the outside world from the people who came to our valley.

The ability to resist some criticism, to stand against the conventional modes of thought, and to tolerate high levels of alienation and personal frustration seem to characterize those who are among the first from their primary groups to be educated. Uniformly these respondents spoke of experiencing disruptions with their families and kin groups, and yet they were compelled by the assurance that in spite of these breaks in interpersonal relations they would win respect for their academic achievements:

When I left my village to go to school, the villagers who did not understand the value of an education were sad and critical. They said, "Now you will remain busy with your books and you will not direct the cattle." Then they added: "Of course, once you read books it will not be your job to direct the cattle."

A drive for economic betterment charaterizes those who lift their educational sights. The prospects of a salaried job with an assured income, of improving one's lot and thereby one's family's, of escaping old fates, of leaving the village and living in the town or city, all support the drive for more education.

Yet the town and the city, for a number of the respondents, was not the end for which education is the means. The goal was to return to the village, to maintain a nice bungalow in it, to enjoy the respect accorded the literate and educated, perhaps to improve the village, but above all to reunite with the kin group in a position of acceptance and influence:

Why do the villagers send their boys to my school? I would not be justified in telling you that they come here to get an education for its own sake. The people here on the frontier connect things like railroads, electricity, telephones, and dams with education. Like you in the West they are coming to associate education with prosperity. They recognize education for its economic value.

Educational aspiration for these respondents found its source in a strong parent, educated model, and economic motivation, and its fulfillment was emotionally supported by the hope for acceptance and influence within the primary reference group.

The desire of the parent to see his child educated is apparently marked by doubt and frustration. That the child will grow away from the parent is sensed, if not fully understood, in these situations where families as closely knit groups provide social warmth and cohesion. That the child will no longer work with his hands if he is educated, thus depriving the family of his much-needed labor, that the community may think of the child as worthless and the parents' decision unwise are all strong possibilities. Yet the decision is made. If the prospects of a well-paying job are perceived to lie beyond education, these doubts may be overcome:

What does a boy do who wants to move upward? Well, if he wants to get a good and decent job, he will go to school; and if he does, he will never be interested in walking behind the buffalo again. Even if he takes work in agriculture, he won't work with his hands. He will get a job with the government.

There is a common story which goes around that a man was asked how many children he had. He said he had four but three were left. When he was asked what happened to the fourth, he said, "He got an education."

The parents' decision to send a son to school is bitter-sweet.

The Response of Elite Groups

Yes, these low-class youngsters are learning new trades and skills in vocational schools like this one. And we're putting a lot of money into these polytechnics; but if I had my way, I would send them to a school where they would learn to keep clean, speak well, and act civilized. Then I would be happy.

Elite groups, in whose hands rest the control of education, are required to respond in some manner to the upward educational thrusts of nonelite persons. These interviews gave me a new appreciation for the complexity of the attitudes surrounding elite responses to the educational demands of the masses.

These responses can be understood only in terms of the social and economic climate in which they arise. The economy is one of scarcity and the society is characterized by rigid class lines which are made no less rigid by long tradition and the sanctions of time. Admitting more people to the educated class inevitably threatens to disturb economic and social class arrangements. Education makes people discontent with low estate and brings to view for the first time the possibility of achieving a higher one:

The upper three percent who run the country want to keep the illiteracy situation the way it is now. They like it that way and they gain an advantage if it continues that way. They want to continue to be an elite and not have a large number of people who can read.

In an economy of scarcity, what is possessed is tightly possessed, whether it be money, position, or power. It is usually hard-won, passed from generation to generation, and elaborate modes of behavior distinguish the rich from the poor. Persons who possess economic power develop keen sensitivity about threats to it, and even though the threats may not be direct or personal they are perceived as though they were.

Economic position and power reserve for the holder a place of privilege in the social structure. This, too, is held with tenacity. It assures deference from those in subordinate positions, proper recognition from equals, and the possibility of preferment from those above:

These village boys who go off to be educated—they no longer show proper respect for zamindars like myself. The last village boy who went to school came back with an improper attitude. He looked into my eyes when he spoke to me, instead of at the ground as he should have.

The zamindars, or landlords, are especially opposed to education for the people. If the people are educated, they say, then they can write applications and letters and stir up trouble. They will create a revolution. Many zamindars say: "Let us let sleeping dogs lie. Let the Bedouins sleep."

Many say that educated people just make more demands upon us and then where will we be? Why should we have more people who will raise more demands when demands are already greater than we are able to take care of? Further, educated people say that when other people are educated, especially the villagers, they will not respect us.

The desire to be educated on the part of those in lower socioeconomic ranks poses the threat of both economic and social competition to elite groups. Yet it is they who control education, and who must ultimately determine the rate at which educational opportunity is extended:

My six years on the subcontinent convince me of the high resistance to bringing schools among the peasants. This resistance comes from above and not from the peasants themselves. But since it is those in elite positions who must bring schools to the villages if they are to have them, the changes must come from above rather than from below; though I have noticed that those on top now are having to be more responsive to what's being thought about at the bottom.

In spite of the implications of these responses, elite opposition to education does not commonly take an open and frontal form. Direct opposition is apparently associated only with the more conservative of elite groups.

Opposition to the rapid extension of schooling usually takes more subtle forms. It may express itself in excessive concern for falling academic standards which usually attend the broadening of the base of the school population. It may find expression in student selection devices and in programs designed to reserve the upper reaches of the educational ladder for the "few and the very few."

Perhaps the most dominant view of the elite toward mass education is found in the attitude toward the sources of the new leadership for the nation and how this new leadership should be trained. One elite view is that leadership can flow only from established leadership.

We must have leadership and it will not come from the vulgar masses. It must come from the good families who are the present leaders. That is where it must come from.

The sons of leaders and the best families should be selected to receive superior education and this in separate schools apart from the sons of lower class families:

The landed gentry of our country must retain its leadership, and the private school of which I am principal must help to cultivate this class. Personally, if this class fails I think we have had it. You know we have a new-rich class in this country and they have money but they do not have culture and education. By contrast, the landed gentry has the background and the culture. It is our purpose to produce a graduate in the image of the elite English public schools. There are no Teddy boys here or pointed shoes with buckles. Here we play cricket and tennis and hockey and football and basketball and volleyball. The purpose of all this is to produce our own chaps.

This argument has strong appeal in a nation with a well defined social structure supporting a small elite at the top. Its appeal is further enhanced when the ordinary government schools are of lesser quality. Using government funds to build a few high-quality schools (costing more than a hundred ordinary schools) is justified on the elite-leadership principle and the necessity, in the face of meager resources, to assure the nation of a flow of select and highly trained young men into government, business, and industry:

When the British were here we had a system of excellent residential schools on the subcontinent. These were schools modeled after the British public schools and designed for upper class children who will be the leaders of our future society. Regrettably this was all changed after the War. Many more people are going to school now than ever before and the towns are growing and surrounding the old schools. Once there was a residential school outside the town where there were hostels, playing fields, debating societies, and the classics were studied. I remember all this with great fondness, but it is all changed now. The towns grew around the schools, swallowed up the playing fields, and the school changed and became a vulgar institution.

We must now recapture the value of the residential school which serves the sons of the leaders of our country and where teachers and students live closely together, and everyone carries on games and education. That is why we are building the new public schools for the high class boys.

While the above sentiment was spoken by a high education official, more egalitarian views on education are not without voice:

The educational leaders wish to create an elite in the British tradition and take a small core of young people and train them to lead the masses. Look at the growing favor with which the elite look at the development of the new "public schools" which receive government grants as opposed to the meager funds which the government primary schools receive. These schools spend something like 425 rupees for each boy. In these schools there are eleven kitchen servants for only 150 boys. The treatment which the boys receive there makes them contemptuous of their past and of the common people and they feel that they no longer belong.

In these schools they get six meals per day and then they are apt to react by saying why don't the poor people go out and eat six meals a day too. In these schools they learn to be clean, punctual, and other values associated with the West. As a result they come to say, "We are clean, we are punctual, why doesn't the dirty villager go out and do something to improve his lot?" This is the boy who will become a government officer and then these are the attitudes he will take toward the villagers, and incidentally the attitude which the villagers will take toward him.

The real need of the country is for primary schools in the villages which will give villagers an opportunity to lift themselves, rather than pouring our money into elite schools.

While strong forces among elite groups work to contain and divert educational aspirations, there are countertrends in political action. Where political institutions are sensitive to the demands of citizens, the appeal of education makes itself felt in the councils of the politicians. In many instances no cause has a stronger, more persistent, or appealing voice than that of education. In fact there are instances where one suspects that the siren song of education is too appealing to the politician's ear and someone should say "no" in order to keep educational programs within wise bounds:

The way a politician gets elected here is to promise the people a school for their children. Have you seen the empty plots of land along the roadside with a little sign sticking up through the weeds which says: "Public School." That is the ground which some politician has had designated as a public school site. But there will be no school. There is no money. The politicians know that, but they promise a school anyway.

But one of the strongest forces countering elitest conceptions of education may be that of industrialization:

The small group of industrialists in our country see a connection between education and economic development. Industrial leaders want to hire people who are creative and well educated. Perhaps the biggest boosts for education may come because of demands of industry for intelligent, creative, and educated people.

The growth of the need for technicians is apparently developing a new respect for vocational programs in the schools, and lifting the status of those who work with their hands:

The increased number of schools and students is breaking down local barriers. Previously, weavers, cobblers, oil pressers and farmers were looked down upon but that is now changing and there is a middle class emerging and more people are coming to be alike. More and more students want to join the polytechnic institutes where they learn to work with their hands. There is a rush on technical education. For example, in one of our medium-size cities there are now 34 industries and many people are drawing 300 to 400 rupees per month as technicians. This creates a new demand for technical education. And it is giving us a new class of people with status.

Rising educational aspirations are part of a social class struggle in which those in positions of status and power are challenged by those who are not. The response of the elite may be frontal opposition, but it is more likely to take the form of developing and maintaining educational programs congenial to their social class purposes. On the one hand there are elite schools for the talented and promising boys who tend to come from the upper socioeconomic classes. On the other, there are vocational and technical schools for less academically talented boys from lower socioeconomic classes.

This social class accommodation to rising educational aspirations may, however, actually be contributing to, rather than slowing the rate of social change. The increasing demand for vocational and technical graduates, and their increasing status and pay, is creating a new elite with economic power. Time favors the new elite. The growing demand for people with specialized and technical competence suggests that the power of this group will wax while that of the older elites will wane.

Closely connected to changes within the social structure and education's linkage to these changes are changes in the control of education. We turn to this matter now.

Challenges to the Control of Education

In the American tradition of local control, we place public schools in the hands of an agency in the community, usually a school board, which represents the higher reaches of community status and power. The day-to-day operations of the school usually rest with teachers and administrators who represent the middle ranges of status and power. Parents of the lower class children tend to be without representation in educational decisions and frequently do not avail themselves of such legal power as they possess, for example the vote in school board elections. In spite of the reluctance of lower classes to assert themselves in school matters in America, participation within a vastly decentralized system is broadly based, though not as broad as many would like.

In the developing countries it is not inevitable that the consumers of education should continue to lack a voice in its control. As expanding opportunities lift educational levels, and educated people are linked to expanding democratic institutions, we may expect that new voices will be heard in the councils of education.

Parents who desire to send their children to school will seek out and influence those elected or appointed officials who can help them. The testimony of the respondents indicates that this pressure from parents to provide ever better educational facilities for children is mounting.

The political appeal of education, as we suggested earlier, has not escaped the politician. A number of times I was reminded that "no politician in his right mind would come out against education." In fact, a sure way to be elected is to promise a school for every child of every constituent:

The politicians are putting lots of pressure on for more schools because they think they are expressing the desire of the villagers for more education. It is quite an experience to come to the capital after working in the villages and to hear all the talk about what a great catastrophe it would be if education cannot be provided for all those who are demanding it. The administration definitely feels that it is being pushed by the politicians to do things that it simply is unable to handle. Here it is commonly said that everything would be well if only the politicians wouldn't whip up this interest in education.

The absolute control of education is gradually slipping from the hands of the professionals. Government officials are finding it politically wise to advocate the extension of educational opportunity and a greater voice in educational affairs. Ministries of education, long used to unchallenged control of education, are finding themselves more and more on the defensive, and other groups, within and without government, are challenging existing ways of doing business in education.

Some of this challenge is coming from new, young leadership in the villages:

I am a village leader. I am young for this position, but my fellow villagers respect me. I am a matriculate, but I do not speak your language.

Some of us in the village thought our school should have a library and books. So we went to the teacher of our village school and told him of our plan. He was not happy with us. He said that the school was his business and the village was our business. We said that he taught our children and we wanted a better school with a library. Further, we would help build the library. He said it was true that he taught our children, but we are not, because of that, his boss. His boss is the inspector of schools in the city, not parents. We went away sad, but we said to him that we would come back to talk about the library again.

Much of the new challenge to the control of education is due to a growing political awareness as well as the willingness to use political power:

In previous times the Minister of Education and other education officials could be oblivious to what people were thinking and saying about education. If they were invited to a meeting they would simply say they were too busy with finance and other matters to come. But now they pay more attention to the requests of people because a person can say, "Look, I have a vote now and if you want to be Minister you will need my vote." Previously, however, the Minister of Education was the least interested in education. Even now, education has little power, but at least Ministers have become interested in the poor primary teachers and are helping children.

Rising educational aspirations and achievement, coupled with growing opportunities for democratic action, are subjecting educational policy and practice to ever closer scrutiny by ever widening segments of the population. The challenge to attitudes of exclusive management in education seems quite clear, and it is requiring considerable value reorientation on the part of those responsible for the administration of education.

The Preservation of Cultural Identity

Up to this point in our inquiry, we have examined the changing social context of education. Now we shall turn to matters quite directly related to the process of education in the schools and rising educational aspirations.

The cultural identity which parents and new students feel for their local institutions and thoughtways is one of their most treasured possessions. Insofar as the schools become agencies for diluting the child's attachments to the cultural patterns of his family and community, or alienate him from them, education becomes an instrument of emotional conflict.

What effect is education perceived to have upon the traditional values and attitudes of youth? Conservative villagers are likely to view the outside values symbolized in the school as threats to their cultural identity. They are not happy about the prospect of their children absorbing values which they do not understand and which they are likely to regard as alien and even irreligious. If the decision on schooling were to be made solely on a value basis, they would probably reject education out of hand.

Villagers do admire the symbols of affluence possessed by educated people and may even desire them for themselves, but they would prefer to acquire them without threat to their cultural values. To the degree, then, that the schools transmit what is regarded as alien values, villagers are ambivalent about them. On the other hand, to the degree to which the school is perceived as an agency for improving their economic position, for enlarging their rights and defending them, they will support it.

The disparity in cultural orientations between the village parent and the educator deserves comment. The educator, be he local village teacher or national planner, comes from a more cosmopolitan tradition, and is likely to identify with national values and norms, while the villager identifies with those of his family, village and kin group.

Local teachers tend to come not from the lower, but the middle classes. They have been educated, not in the village, but in the town or city. Their own teachers in the training colleges came out of a Western, cosmopolitan tradition. Many of the books they read were Western books. Their training has effectively socialized them away from their humble beginnings, if that is where they began.

The national planners similarly are not concerned about the preservation of local folkways. They are concerned about the need for "national integration" through education, for building loyalties to symbols of nationhood, the constitution, national heroes, art, literature, music, and political leaders:

The main purpose of village education is not so much to teach reading and writing as to let villagers know that they are a part of a nation state.

Some national planners in education feel that something bad will happen if the Pathans speak only Pashto. I say, however, that people are happiest when their homes and hearts are safe. It is our religion that holds us together and also local customs and traditions, but the government is not tolerant of this point of view. They feel that the Pathans must be brought into a national orientation. On the other hand, the Pathans feel that the government is trying to curb their native customs.

The villager views the school in more limited terms than either the local teacher or the national planner, and more pragmatically. He hopes simply that his child will resist the alien influences of the school while acquiring the tools necessary to make a better livelihood for himself and the family. He wants to preserve his family and his culture as he understands it. It can be a better culture if his son is educated and succeeds.

Upper class parents, in contrast to villagers, may want their children to embrace Westernized values, but here too there is ambivalence:

Some parents, especially those in the upper and middle classes, are happy to have their children competing for the symbols of status which characterize Western elites. But competition for the symbols of Western eliteness is not without conflict. Parents with a Western orientation are interested in having their students move up, and gain satisfaction in having them do so. They want, thereby, to achieve an eliteness for themselves, as well as for their children. Their reference group is the elite, Westernized group.

But at the same time the pull of tradition on the parents is there, and frequently Western type schools are approved with a disapproval. There is the feeling that children are not learning Islamic values but rather are moving with the times. In the middle urban class, education is required for status, but it does not lead to peace of mind and soul.

The focal point of the cultural identity problem is the student. He comes to school from a family interested in preserving its identity within the local group. His teacher is more than likely a representative of a national culture. Between these opposing cultural identifications he is expected to learn his lessons:

The real break for the village boy comes in high school. Up to that time schooling has kept him pretty much identified with the village, but at high school things begin to change as he starts to learn values which are different from his own. At this point, it is likely that the village boy will look down upon the villagers and break with them.

The village schools are very much divorced from village life. They have little impact upon the village. Education there does not train children to see and appreciate local environment.

The student's indigenous language and family background turn him toward a rejection of the school's cultural identification and toward a reaffirmation of his own. Other forces tear him in opposite directions. If he achieves in school, the very act of achievement thrusts him away from the village to seek his fortune in the city. He probably knows early in his schooling that his ultimate destination is outside the village and this knowledge causes him increasingly to identify with the larger culture symbolized by the school. When he returns from school to his home, he carries this knowledge in his head, and there he confronts, as he did in school, the necessity of reconciling within himself to the pull of opposing cultural identifications:

Western style education has separated most of us from our own culture. We are what you might call "divided men." Our education undermined our family relationships which are traditional and have historic sanction. It did not undermine family relationships directly, but indirectly. It did not teach directly that family relationships should be broken, but it had that effect nevertheless. For example, the schools teach the importance of less emotional, more rational, relationships. It teaches that a father is just another man. It teaches more individualism. Our family, on the other hand, is tied together by strong emotional ties and is mutually dependent upon itself. As a result of all this when I went out of my village, I began to dislike my village and to think of the people who brought me up as illiterate and foolish.

The respondents offered two interpretations of the school as an agent for changing cultural identifications. One was that the change is a painful, though necessary, part of nation building, of bringing cohesion to heterogeneous groups, of welding them into a nation-state. The school is the ideal institution for bringing about this higher level of values and orientation.

The other group of respondents found values worth preserving in local cultures and urged that the school should be an instrument in helping villagers discriminate between useful and nonuseful values. This view was expressed by former President S. Radhakrishnan:

We must find ways to bring change to the village without taking people out of the village, and the school can help do this. It is better to bring the amenities to the village than the villager to the city, where he is shut off from all that is meaningful to him.

And the school can help to make the village meaningful to the child if the fine traditions are passed along to the child, the stories, the sayings, the dramas, the heroic epics. This moral and social aspect of the child's education makes for greater difference in the long run than the three R's.

Discontinuities Between Home and School

Problems of cultural identification are frequently acute because of the discontinuities that exist between the home and the school. We now examine certain aspects of these discontinuities. A number of respondents reminded me that "in early times" education was a unified process, a melding of the common aspirations and values of home and school:

Education was a part of life and there was no necessity for bridging the gap between the school and life around it. It was related functionally and totally. However, it is different now with modern education. Whereas the early teacher, the guru, was a spiritual father, the modern teacher is only a secular father. There was an early saying that the bones of the child belonged to the father and the flesh to the teacher. In other words, the teacher was free to do with the child as he wished. Now teachers are divorced from what is happening around the school.

The reasons for the increasing discontinuity between the home and the school are attributed to trends toward secularization in modern life, the breakdown of homogeneous communities, and increasing specialization in economic activities.

Discontinuities between the home and the school show themselves in different ways. For example, they are seen in the attempts of some teachers to be more democratic in their relations with students who come from authoritarian homes. Such attempts may create in the mind of the child serious conflicts about the proper relationship between a child and an adult. Sometimes the discontinuities are apparent in the subject matter of the schools if it runs contrary to village folkways and beliefs. The clash is between a rational and a folk culture:

In high school, students are taught that drinking water contains certain contaminating bacteria and that water in the village well will likely be contaminated and should be boiled before it is drunk. A high school boy who returns to his village from the school will have to make a decision to listen to his teacher or to his fellow villagers. I predict that in this and in most cases he will listen to the villagers because they are more influential than the teacher.

I remember, for example, a boy that I knew who went to high school and who was also a member of the village where I was visiting. I had with me a thermos jug and the boy asked me why I carried a thermos jug. I told him because it was clean and the water was boiled. The boy then commented that village water was not contaminated. Rather, it has minerals which machinery and metals, such as pumps, take out. He commented that this was a village belief and that while he thought it was inaccurate he felt compelled to believe it.

The discontinuities between home and school may lead to parent-child estrangement, especially if the child embraces the new values symbolized in the school, and becomes upwardly mobile:

The daughter of an illiterate mother I know went into nursing. The daughter is now ashamed of the mother and the mother seems to share this same feeling of shame regarding the new life of her daughter. This daughter, by virtue of the fact that she had achieved an education, has taken on a new set of social values which are no longer compatible with those of her mother.

Or, take the example of the son of my tonga driver, who is now educated. The position of the father, of course, is much lower than that of the son. The social distinction between them now is so great that the father does not even wish to see his son for fear that others would know that his father is a tonga walla.

Yet, it is these upwardly mobile persons who are forming the new middle class, as suggested by the same respondent who made the above comments:

The real breakup comes after matriculation, and these persons who do not go on to college form a new middle class consisting of teachers, clerks, junior grade level government clerks, and servants. They are forming a new social class and this new social class is having a tremendous impact upon the family. It has an impact on the personal relationships within the family, which at one time was close knit but which now is breaking up. Education disturbs the close relationship between children and parents. The nurse, for example, about whom I spoke a moment ago, would not like to have her mother come visit her even though her mother wished to go. On the other hand, the daughter is trying to get her brothers and sisters out of low jobs and into high jobs.

There was a growing feeling among the teachers to whom I spoke that the gulf between the school and the home had to be bridged somehow. There was a genuine desire to apply what had been learned in training colleges and in in-service courses. Yet there is doubt about whether it can be accomplished.

Another factor in the discontinuity between home and school is the fact that the teacher's primary professional reference group is not in the community. It is, rather, in the educational bureaucracy located in a district or divisional headquarters. The future of his career is tied to the bureaucracy, which decides his salary and promotions. The bureaucracy judges him in part by how many of his students pass the standardized examination. In fact his salary increments may be tied to the number of passes his students receive. He, therefore, focuses his attention and energies on devising methods for getting his students to pass examinations.

The teacher's link to the educational bureaucracy is intensified by his isolation within the school setting. His social and professional roles within the school are stylized. His relations with the headmaster must be correct and restrained or he will be given a bad report when the inspector visits the schools. With the inspector he must be properly subservient:

I was teaching my middle school class when the inspector came in. Looking at me, he said, "I am the deputy inspector; what do you teach?"
"I teach English," I said.
"Then show me your time table."
I then moved over near to where the inspector stood so that I could reach for the time table which was posted on the wall. I took it down from the wall and as I did so my sleeve brushed the clothing of the inspector. The inspector stood up to his full height immediately and said, "Don't you know who I am? Aren't you aware of the fact that I am the deputy inspector?"
I replied that I did know that he was the deputy inspector, and that I was sorry that I brushed his clothes. But the inspector was incensed and he started to quiz my class, but my boys were perfect and they answered the questions well.

While this was going on, I saw the headmaster standing outside in the hall and peeking in on the class. Then the inspector said, "Why have you done this work for the second term, when this is only the first term?" I said that I had explained to the headmaster that my boys had already done the first term's work and that we were working ahead. The headmaster just sat outside listening and when we were finished and the inspector had gone, the headmaster called me and he said: "Why did you quarrel with him? Why didn't you keep him happy?"

The children sense quite early that the teacher is a stranger in their midst, and he is left quite alone without really satisfying links with students, the community, or the educational bureaucracy. Thus the one person who could effectively change discontinuity between home and school into continuity is rendered helpless to do so.

Peer Groups

Students of school systems point out how the schools tend to foster the growth of the peer groups among children of similar ages. The peer society may organize itself around values which are quite at variance with those espoused by either the teachers and administration or the parents. The strength of the peer group in respect to the purposes of the school seems to be in direct relation to the strength of the linkage which exists between the home and the school. In situations where the parents feel estranged from the operations of the school and have little contact with it, the peer group is free to develop with minimum control and direction from either parents or school personnel. On the other hand, where there is strong linkage between the home and the school, the peer group is less likely to be disruptive of school operations and purposes.

The development of peer groups within the schools of developing countries is influenced by these factors, plus conditions which are unique to given situations. The traditional respect for adult authority, for example, may be transferred from the family to the teacher and thus slow the development of a distinct peer society. Other conditions in the developing countries, however, stimulate the rapid development of youth cultures. With the extension of educational opportunity, the schools assume more responsibility for the full socialization of the child and the assimilation of minority class children into the dominant culture. These goals become in effect a challenge to the authority and wisdom of the parent generation.

The parent generation in some instances has at least limited control over what happens in the school. In many cases, however, the actual control of the school resides in distant cities. In such case the school lacks both the social control of the family and that of its own authority. The peer group fills the vacuum.

Where the local school does exercise effective social control, the teacher frequently inculcates values, customs, and thoughtways at variance or in conflict with those of the elders. In the middle are the pupils, cut loose for the time being from the authority of the family and uncommitted to that of the teacher. The situation invites the development of peer group attitudes and values:

I talk to a number of secondary school girls each year. I say to them, "Why is the younger generation so misunderstood and why do you say that you are misunderstood? In what ways are you misunderstood?" These girls talk to me for a long time but they do not know what they want. There are many things they don't want, but in terms of the things they do want they aren't very sure. The one thing that they do want is freedom from their parents. This is completely new among our children. One girl said to me, "In your generation you just sat nodding to your father; we won't do that." These girls are estranged from their own culture.

With my own children I am always ending up in a fight and I know it is because I represent one set of values and they represent another. These children are getting unlimited freedom in the schools and this unlimited freedom of the young means that they are reading different things, they are seeing movies with foreign and strange ideas, they are listening to radios which bring strange ideas, and they are exposed to great influences which we were not exposed to. What I resent most is that this upsets the economy of our house. I have to alter all of the clothes and make sacrifices myself in order to accommodate the whims of my daughter.

The rise of peer groups apparently is altering the social systems of the schools by introducing a third force to the traditional teacher-parent polarity. This new force is increasingly independent of the other two and seems destined in the future to have a substantial impact upon the school learning process.

Classroom Learning Climate

When the schools of the developing countries were more selective than they are now and more shaply focused in their academic purposes, the motivation of students was supported in the family and kin group and by the prospect of employment in a status position. These students came from families with proud traditions in the Western type of education, and they were surrounded from early childhood with cultural incentives toward education. Many of them spoke English more easily than their native tongue and were acquainted even before going to school with English history and literature.

The new generation of students are strangers to these traditions which were nourished among the elite of the colonial nation. To what extent do they find motivation to achieve in schools which have in many ways remained unchanged in their curriculum and patterns of organization from colonial days?

As teachers we are conscientiously trying to educate everybody, but how can we do it with all of them? How can you handle in one room all these children of such different abilities and backgrounds? It used to be that we had select groups and the teacher could maintain standards. Now just anyone comes. They aren't interested in learning. Wouldn't it be better to use our meager resources on those few who are in a position to profit by what we have to teach?

Apparently little systematic effort has been made to find out exactly what it is that the new generations of parents and students expect to receive from education, or how they visualize the role which education can play in their lives. Nor has much been done to adapt curriculum programs to the new conditions of mass education.

The curriculum to which these children are exposed is a standardized national or state one, handed down from central planning agencies in urban centers. It is assumed that what will work in one setting will automatically work in another:

Now that all the children are being admitted, examination standards are falling and we seem to be no farther ahead than we were before. Many principals and headmasters have said to me that standards have been falling for ten years and we expect that they will continue to so long as young people come in such large numbers. They regret the fact that they have to accept people who are not qualified in their own terms.

If the planners were thoroughly familiar with village culture and if there was a willingness to experiment and improvise, there might be developed educational programs, materials, and techniques that would result in higher rates of achievement. As it is now, many students apparently find the gulf between local culture and national curricula too difficult to bridge. The very high dropout rates, especially in the early years of school, would suggest that the student has great difficulty in making the transition:

I told my students that I did not know who sent our curriculum and they did not know why they were to study my subject, but that they just had to study and I had to teach.

For ten years I am there and no one once consulted me about my teaching. I am just handed the curriculum and told to teach it.

High rates of failure on standardized materials and tests depresses the learning climate in the classroom and creates mutual distrust among teachers and students. The teachers come to believe that children with lowly backgrounds are so lacking in culture that they cannot achieve academically. The children are apt to regard the teacher and his subject matter as foreign and hence legitimate targets for indifference and even hostility. Such destructive emotions absorb energies which would otherwise be available for learning:

Most of our wastage comes from the new arrivals from the lower classes. Those who come from the upper classes know how to achieve in school, but children from the lower classes do not.

Summary and Conclusions

The first conclusion to be drawn from this investigation relates to the first assumption, namely that rising educational aspirations constitute a new social force in education with far-reaching consequences. The interviews left me with the dominant impression that this single variable flows through the education process like a dye, coloring all that it touches. The impression is gained that some of the energies now consumed in meeting the shortages caused by rising educational aspirations—money, teachers, buildings, and instructional materials—might profitably be diverted toward learning more about how this new social force influences the conditons of learning and how it can be used constructively. Attention to the prime cause may enable planners to use more strategically those elements in education which are in short supply.

The first hypothesis regarding the impact of rising educational expectations and achievement on the control of education is affirmed by the data from these interviews. There is evidence of rising demands for changes in education and these demands are associated with, if not caused by, the increasing pressure for schooling. Educational establishments are being placed in defensive positions as the voices for change mount in intensity. There seems to be arising a new sensitivity to popular demands for education, spurred on by growing political participation.

The second hypothesis asserted that under the influence of mass education the goals of the school will shift toward the full socialization of the child and the assimilation of children of "deviant" ethnic and social backgrounds. This seems actually to be taking place, but as a side product of schooling, rather than as a main goal. Local administrators and teachers are likely to complain about "all these different children in the schools," and the difficulty they confront under the circumstances of "maintaining standards." There seems to be no coherent or sustained policy for socializing the child or integrating him into the dominant culture.

The problem of local teachers and administrators is likely to be a reflection of ambivalence in aims at the top of the education hierarchy. On the one hand there is the drive to use the schools to give "emotional integration" to heterogeneous groups, to "Indianize" the young generation. On the other hand, there is the effort to maintain standardized levels of academic achievement among children of great diversity of background and academic orientation. The two goals create tension and confusion about what the schools should accomplish with children.

It is gratifying to note, however, the extent to which schools generally are assimilating children of vastly different social class backgrounds. These schools seem to be fulfilling the "melting pot" function served historically by American schools with immigrant populations.

The extent to which schools are assimilating heterogeneous populations indicates their growing influence as social institutions, the fourth hypothesis. These interviews would suggest that educators are only now beginning to regard the schools as social institutions capable of serving worthy social purposes. While in practice they are broadening their social purposes, the recognition that they are is only now beginning to catch hold. The earlier image of the school as an elite institution with narrowly academic and intellectual purposes persists into the era of growing mass education. Attempts to reconcile the earlier image with the realities of the present is a source of considerable soul searching among both the suppliers and consumers of education.

Closely associated with the school's social role is the third hypothesis regarding the rise of peer groups. The evidence indicates that their formation is a new and little understood phenomenon in the more traditional areas. There is a widening impression that school-age children "are not obedient to their parents as they used to be," and that teachers "no longer command respect" as they did before. The interviews presented no evidence, however, on a matter of considerable interest, namely the impact of peer values on school learning.

Hypothesis five, regarding the response of elite groups to pressures for mass education, is fully affirmed by the interview data. As nearly as I can ascertain, the broadening socioeconomic base of the educational pyramid in developing countries is seldom analyzed from the viewpoint of social class conflict and change. Yet, to be fully understood, it must be seen in these terms.

In the long view I would regard the present programs of elite education as serving a transitional phase between earlier periods when education was the exclusive property of a small elite and future periods when public education hopefully will be of higher quality and appeal than it is now. New leadership from the bottom, uninitiated in the elitist conception of education, is likely to have considerable influence in the future change.

Hypothesis six asserts that the extension of mass education will accentuate the cultural discontinuity between the home and the school. The school as an exclusive institution in an earlier day could establish harmonious continuity with its exclusive clientele. The cultures, represented by each, meshed. This is no longer true. The school has itself become a more heterogeneous organization serving a far more heterogeneous clientele. Further, the school is now regarded frankly as a vehicle for upward mobility. The exclusive schools of an earlier day *began* with children of the elite classes. They educated them to keep and appreciate their high station. Today's schools—at least many of them—begin with children of low station who have their eyes on a higher one. They are instruments of social change. Discontinuity is built into their role.

The crucial problem for the school becomes one of handling this new and strange role. If constructive ways are found to articulate new aspirations of worth with old traditions of value, the schools of the developing countries will enter upon a new and exciting era of social usefulness.

5

The Social Psychology of Heterogeneous Schools

Thomas F. Pettigrew and Patricia J. Pajonas

In this chapter Thomas Pettigrew and Patricia Pajonas assert that certain forces in the modern world dramatically increase intermingling across cultural lines. There is reason to believe that this trend toward heterogeneity will accelerate rather than diminish. Yet most of our schools are homogeneous in their group composition. Should they be? Can homogeneous schools teach students to live in a heterogeneous world? How do homogeneous and heterogeneous school situations influence students within them? Are the influences beneficial or harmful? To get at questions like these, Pettigrew and Pajonas review an array of empirical research drawn from a number of sources. Through a careful weighing of available evidence they are able to indicate what we do know about these questions and what we need yet to find out.

The past generation in world history has witnessed many remarkable changes, but none more remarkable than the mass destruction of barriers to intergroup contact. The global scale of World War II, the end of colonialism, the expansion of literacy, the speed of urbanization, the scope of mass migrations, the growth of rapid transportation, and the proliferation of the mass media—these and other interrelated processes have led in recent years to more intermingling across class, cultural, tribal, racial, religious, regional, and national lines than ever previously imagined. Indeed, this book itself is both a product and a symbol of this worldwide phenomenon.

There is no reason to anticipate an abatement of these sweeping changes; rather, there is every reason to expect a continuation and even an acceleration of this trend toward increasing group heterogeneity. Yet most formal education takes place in situations of group homogeneity. Thus the question arises: Are unigroup schools an insufficient, even harmful, preparation for today's and especially tomorrow's world?

This chapter tentatively answers "yes" to this query. The explorative discussion which follows asserts that a heterogeneous world demands heterogeneous training. More precisely, the authors consider the following hypothesis: *The more comparable the intergroup learning situation and the intergroup performance situation, the better the later retention and performance.* Such a broad-gauged hypothesis requires careful testing, qualification, and further specification. In lieu of an extensive literature directed squarely at these tasks, however, this paper approaches the problem with empirical data and theoretical considerations drawn from a variety of related research realms ranging from human verbal learning to the effects of various social class climates in schools.

Human Verbal Learning Research

We can begin our exploration with a series of early studies on human retention of verbal material. Social changes in the learning context can impair recall performance. One study noted that when the initial learning took place without an audience, the presence of a small audience during relearning decreased retention.[1] And another investigation found that under normal classroom conditions recall was diminished when either the classroom or the proctor in the original learning situation was changed.[2] Indeed, even further impairment resulted when both the classroom and the proctor were changed.

Case illustrations support these laboratory findings in a variety of real life settings. A number of such cases involve the return of language skills once the individual is reestablished in the locale where the language was originally learned. Other examples report the sudden return of childhood memories when individuals reenter their childhood environments.[3]

These data support at a basic learning level our central hypothesis: the more comparable the learning situation is with the performance situation, the better the later retention and performance.[4] Two processes underlie this principle. Altered conditions deter performance, in part because the old stimuli necessary to elicit the originally learned acts are not effectively present, and in part because new stimuli are introduced that evoke responses which compete with the originally learned acts.

The extension of this learning principle to the school environment assumes: (1) that the group differentiation in question is salient for the children; and (2) that group heterogeneity will characterize the adult lives of the children. When these assumptions are justified—as they are for a vast and growing segment of the world's youth—then the reasoning behind intergroup schooling becomes straightforward. For optimal performance as adults, continuity in intergroup experiences between the school and later life becomes mandatory.

Social Psychological Work on Small Groups

The Biracial Research of Katz

Human beings educated in homogeneous social settings generally feel awkward and ill at ease and evince lowered performance when later placed in heterogeneous settings. Research on black Americans by Irwin Katz is especially relevant here.[5] First, Katz studied biracial task groups consisting of two black and two white students. In a variety of conditions, the black subjects "displayed marked social inhibition and subordination to white partners." Long accustomed to all black situations, the blacks made fewer remarks than did whites, tended to accept the whites' contributions uncritically, ranked whites higher on intellectual performance even after equal racial ability had been displayed, and later expressed less satisfaction with the group experience than did whites.

These compliant tendencies were modified only after a situation was presented which required the black subjects to announce openly correct problem solutions to their white partners. Katz has also demonstrated performance effects of the biracial context on his white subjects. Long accustomed to all-white situations, the white subjects often failed to utilize the abilities of their black partners, even when they could expect a monetary bonus from the experimenter for good teamwork.

A second series of experiments by Katz reveals further effects of racial separation and discrimination by introducing threat into different racial environments. Thus students at a predominantly black college in the southern United States performed better on a digit-symbol substitution task under conditions of low stress when tested by a white stranger, but under conditions of high stress when tested by a black stranger. Likewise, black students in another experiment scored higher on a digit-symbol code with a white tester as long as they believed the code to be a research instrument for studying hand-eye coordination—a nonintellectual capacity; but they did much better with a black tester when they thought the code was an intelligence measure.

Katz has also isolated some of the effects upon black Americans of anticipated comparison with white Americans. Students at a black college in the southern United States worked on easy and difficult versions of a digit-symbol task under three different instructions: one set of instructions described the task as not being a test at all, another set described it as a scholastic aptitude test with norms from the black college itself, and a third set described it as a scholastic aptitude test with national (i.e., predominantly white) college norms. The black subjects performed best when they anticipated comparison with other blacks, less well when they anticipated comparison with whites, and least well when no comparison at all was anticipated.

Another study again varied the anticipated comparison with whites or other blacks, but at the same time varied conditions of white or black experimenter and different probabilities of success. The results of this experiment are consistent with those just cited. The black subjects performed best when tested by a white with a reasonable expectation (i.e., 60%) of success and anticipation of comparison with black norms; they performed worst when tested by a white with a low expectation (i.e., 10%) of success and anticipation of comparison with white norms.

Katz believes these findings are consistent with a four-factor theory of black American performance in biracial situations. On the negative side of the ledger, he first lists (1) *lowered probability of success*. Where there is marked discrepancy in the educational standards of black and white schools, or where black children have already acquired strong feelings of inferiority, they are likely to have a *low expectancy of academic success* when introduced into integrated classes. This expectancy is often realistic, considering the situation, but it has the effect of lowering achievement motivation. The practical implication of this factor is to avoid its operation by beginning intergroup instruction in the earliest grades.

(2) *Social threat* is involved in any biracial situation for black Americans; because of the prestige and dominance of whites in American society, rejection of black students by white classmates and teachers often elicits emo-

tional responses that are detrimental to intellectual functioning. The practical implication here is that intergroup education is an essential first step, but intergroup acceptance is necessary to fulfill its potential.

(3) *Failure threat* arises when academic failure means disapproval by significant others—parents, teachers, or peers at school. Low expectancy of success under failure threat may also elicit emotional responses detrimental to performance. But this need not always be the case. Sometimes, experiences in the intergroup classroom act to dispel feelings of failure threat and group inferiority. When one of the nine black children who, under the glare of world publicity, desegregated Central High School of Little Rock, Arkansas, in 1957 was asked what she had learned from her arduous experience, she exclaimed: "Now I know that there are some stupid white kids, too!"

On the positive side of the ledger, Katz notes that acceptance of blacks by white classmates and teachers has (4) *a social facilitation effect* upon their ability to learn, apparently because it reassures black children that they are expected to be as talented in the classroom as anyone else. This anticipation, that skillful performance will win white approval rather than rejection for not "knowing his place," endows scholastic success with *high incentive value.* Katz believes this factor explains why his black subjects perform better with white investigators on tasks which are free of severe threat.

In summary, then, the intergroup learning situation involving groups of traditionally different status has the potentiality of lowering or raising performance, depending to a considerable extent on the social context of threat or acceptance that is achieved. Important, too, is the fact that all four of Katz's factors—lowered probability of success, social threat, failure threat, and social facilitation—are processes that are likely to result from separation for any low-status group in any society.

Other Small Group Research

Additional relevant research on small groups considers the effects of group heterogeneity and homogeneity. To begin with, similarity of attitudes, values, and interests is an important and effective basis for the natural formation of cohesive social groups. Hence, Theodore Newcomb found such similarity to be a critical factor in the establishment of three cliques in the natural setting of a college student residence.[6] And research on marital happiness indicates that similarity of interests and attitudes is conducive to a harmonious marriage[7] (conversely, married couples who are happy believe themselves to be similar)[8] Finally, August Hollingshead noted that leisure time activities within socioeconomic classes are in large part shaped by the desire of people to associate with people like themselves.[9] Such data suggest that homogeneity of individual characteristics among members of a group contributes to member satisfaction.

More detailed investigations support this possibility. One study compared creative groups which were either homogeneous or heterogeneous in authoritarian attitudes.[10] The homogeneous groups proved to be more friendly and have higher morale; the heterogeneous groups exhibited more conflict and competition together with a greater tendency toward clique formation.

But greater harmony in homogeneous groups does not necessarily translate into greater productivity. Consider the study by C. C. Pelz of factors influencing the performance of scientists in a research organization.[11] He noted that frequent contact with other scientists was positively related to an individual's productivity only if the contacts were with scientists *unlike* the individual himself in motivation and experience. An analogous phenomenon has been noted by L. R. Hoffman in the laboratory.[12] Hoffman assigned subjects to four-member groups designated as similar or dissimilar on the basis of scores on the Guilford-Zimmerman Temperament Survey. The heterogeneous groups produced significantly superior solutions to a multisolution "mined road" problem and showed a definite tendency to produce more inventive solutions to a human relations problem.

Investigations using different criteria of productivity, however, have sometimes found homogeneous groups to be more effective. II. A. Grace, for example, compared the performance of fourteen high school basketball teams with the homogeneity of the players' self-descriptions.[13] The homogeneity of players' self-descriptions within teams proved to be positively related to the number of games won by the teams (rank order correlation = +.61). In another study, William Schutz organized three types of groups around his concept of a personal vs. counterpersonal personality trait.[14] An individual is regarded as personal or counterpersonal to the extent that he agrees or disagrees with such statements as "I like to talk about myself in a group" and "I like groups where people get personal." Schutz formed homogeneous groups of either all personal or all counterpersonal subjects and heterogeneous groups composed of both types. On a variety of tasks, both the all personal and all counterpersonal groups performed better than the heterogeneous groups.

Clearly, the effects of group composition upon productivity are complex. Three critical questions arise: Homogeneous in what particular characteristics? Heterogeneous in what characteristics? And what are the criteria of group productivity? It appears that both heterogeneity and homogeneity can facilitate group productivity, depending upon the variables involved.

The point is well illustrated by the results of an investigation of 80 ten-men groups on a wide assortment of tasks.[15] Groups which were heterogeneous in the personality traits of surgency, radicalism, character integration, and adventuresomeness tended to render more accurate group judgments. But in these same 80 groups, heterogeneity in sensitivity, suspiciousness, and aggressiveness related to slowness in decision making and the feeling on the part of group members that goal achievement was being blocked.

This small-group research assumes particular interest for educators when it is applied to the popular technique of ability grouping. E. P. Torrance took a controlled look at this issue by studying homogeneous and heterogeneous groupings of young school children working together on a common task.[16] In two schools, homogeneous groups were formed by placing together the five pupils in the class who ranked highest on a measure of creativity, the next five in rank in a second group, etc. In another school the same procedure was followed, using intelligence test rather that creativity test scores to divide the groups. Heterogeneous groups were devised in other classes on the basis of the same tests by taking every fifth student for the first group, etc. Torrance asked all the groups to think of as many uses as possible for a collection of such scientific toys as a magnet and to explain the principle behind these suggested uses. Each group worked for 25 minutes and was watched by a trained observer who recorded instances of positive (e.g., cooperating, organizing, praising one another) and negative (e.g., bickering, dominating, not cooperating) interactions.

The findings of this ability grouping research are consistent with other small group studies. In each school, the number of positive interactions was significantly greater in the homogeneous groups. But, once again, positive group actions did not translate directly into effective group action, for the homogeneous groups of children were not more productive. In fact, the greater degree of tension in the heterogeneous groups may actually have stimulated the general motivational level and fostered significant contributions to the group.

Evidence indicates that these small-group findings apply in part to intergroup classrooms. Thus, R. W. Pugh found that students in an all-black school were somewhat more relaxed and better adjusted to school life than black students in an interracial school, though the two groups did not differ in "race pride."[17] But the segregated youngsters were less satisfied with their school administrators and teachers. Recent research in Michigan schools confirms this tension in some biracial classrooms.[18] Another study of a desegregated summer camp also noted tension and keen sensitivity among black children, much of which centered around fears of rejection by the white campers.[19] Two weeks of successful integration, however, achieved a sharp decline in this initial black sensitivity.

To sum up, one recurrent characteristic of heterogeneous groups is their greater tension and conflict. Yet this characteristic does not necessarily prevent these groups from generally being as productive as homogeneous groups. Indeed, some research suggests that high level creativity and particular tasks may best be achieved in heterogeneous groups.

Social Psychological Work on Intergroup Contact

Allport's Four Contact Conditions for Intergroup Acceptance

Intergroup classrooms per se need not arouse low expectancy of academic success, social and failure threat, and tension. Nor must they remain "heterogeneous groups" at all. An intergroup classroom is heterogeneous only so long as the group identifications of the students persist as dominant features of the classroom. The disadvantages of biracial and heterogeneous groups suggested by small-group research can be minimized by a growing intergroup acceptance generated by the classroom situation itself. And the socially facilitating effects of mixed groups noted by Katz, Pelz, and Hoffman can be maximized by this same growth of acceptance.

The evolution of intergroup acceptance through contact, however, is more complex than dictated by conventional wisdom. Many well meaning people believe that if only conflicting groups could experience more contact with each other, the world's intergroup difficulties would solve themselves. Unfortunately, the case is not so simple. Africans and Europeans have more contact in the Republic of South Africa than anywhere else, Muslims and Hindus more contact in India and Pakistan, and black and white Americans more contact in the southern United States; yet none of these areas is conspicuous for its intergroup harmony. It almost appears as if contact between two peoples exacerbates, rather than relieves, intergroup hostility.

Yet this conclusion is as hasty and fallacious as the assumption that contact invariably lessens prejudice. Increasing interaction of groups or individuals intensifies and magnifies the processes already underway. Consequently, more intergroup contact can lead either to greater prejudice and rejection or to greater respect and acceptance, depending upon the situation in which it occurs. The basic issue, then, concerns the *types of situations* in which contact leads to trust or distrust.

Gordon Allport, in his review of the relevant research, concludes that four characteristics of the contact situation are of the utmost importance.[20] Prejudice is lessened when the two groups in contact: (1) possess equal status, (2) seek common goals, (3) are cooperatively dependent upon each other, and (4) interact with the positive support of authorities, laws, or custom.

Contact between groups of contrasting social status may do little more than reinforce old and hostile stereotypes. In the typical South African situation of interracial contact, for example, most Africans encountered by Europeans are servants and other low status workers. Many Europeans eventually conclude that these are the jobs best suited for Africans, that somehow this is the African's "proper place." To be sure, there are African professionals in South Africa, but *apartheid* has forced them to stay deep within the African world where Europeans rarely meet them. The white supremacist who boasts that he "really knows the native" is usually referring to his casual encounters with Africans in which the Africans are socially defined as being of lower status. This is one reason why the plentiful African-European patterns of contact in South Africa have not led to interracial understanding.

Equal-status contact attacks this problem by providing a situation in which groups are defined and treated as being of equal worth. The society may still assign the groups differential status, but the classroom can insist on equal status treatment for all. Such a classroom provides the optimum setting for groups to discover common interests. The importance of discovering similarities across groups is underlined by recent research which suggests that assumed belief conflict is more basic to intergroup prejudice than the group differentiation itself. Hence, recent studies suggest that social distance attitudes toward blacks are less a function of racial prejudice per se than the assumption of many white Americans that black Americans hold dissimilar beliefs and values.[21]

When groups work together toward common goals, further opportunities are presented for developing and discovering similarities of interests and values. The reduction of prejudice through contact generally requires an active, focused effort, not simply a gathering together for the sheer sake of intermingling. This condition of common goals is well understood in several newly independent countries. Needing to develop a unifying spirit of nationhood and to diminish old cultural, religious, or tribal rivalries, many new nations have systematically recruited members from all of the intranational factions into such common goal organizations as the civil service and the armed forces.

Furthermore, the attainment of these common goals must be a mutually dependent effort involving no competition along strictly group lines. Athletic teams furnish pertinent examples. If one rugby team consisted of all Maori New Zealanders and another of all Caucasian New Zealanders, the two teams could probably play indefinitely and not become more racially tolerant. Though equal status and common goal conditions would prevail, the lines of competition would make race relevant. But two mixed teams of both Maori and Caucasian New Zealanders not only create an equal-status contact situation, but one in which the team members cannot achieve their common goal of winning without the assistance of each other. Under such conditions, race and other group distinctions lose importance.

The final factor concerns the auspices of the contact. If the situation has *explicit social sanction,* intergroup contact is more readily accepted and has more positive effects. Though the contact may be a bit awkward at first, authority support helps to make it seem "right."

Field research highlights these contact principles in operation. One study found that white American merchant marines tended to hold racial attitudes in direct relation to how many voyages they had taken with equal-status black American seamen—the more desegregated voyages, the more positive their attitudes.[22] Another investigation noted that white Philadelphia policemen who had personally worked with black colleagues were far more favorable toward the desegregation of their force than other white policemen.[23] A third study of white American government workers, veterans, and students found that those who had know black American professionals were far less prejudiced toward blacks than those who had known only unskilled blacks.[24]

The most solid evidence comes from housing research. Repeated American studies have found that integrated living in public housing developments, which meet all four of Allport's contact criteria, sharply reduces racial prejudice among both black and white neighbors.[25] Contrariwise, living in segregated but otherwise identical housing developments structures interracial contact in such a way that, if anything, racial bitterness is enhanced.

Additional data derive from the racial desegregation of the U. S. Armed Forces.[26] Once again, conditions involving optimal contact led directly to the reduction of racial prejudice among both black and white servicemen.

As a black officer in Korea candidly phrased it: "After a while you start thinking of whites as people."

One important qualification attends attitude change through intergroup contact: at least in the initial stages, the change is often limited to the specific situation involved. Consider an American neighborhood of white steel workers.[27] These men were members of the same thoroughly desegregated union and worked in desegregated plants. In fact, black Americans held elected positions as high officers of the union and shared with whites the same locker rooms, lunch rooms, showers, and toilets in both the union hall and the plants. Only 12 percent of the 151 whites studied evinced "low acceptance" of blacks in this work situation; and the deeper the involvement in union activities, the greater was the white acceptance of blacks as co-workers.

But neighborhood acceptance was a vastly different matter to these men. Bolstered by a neighborhood organization which opposed racial integration, 86 percent of the white steel workers opposed blacks living near them, with those men most involved in the collective existence of the neighborhood expressing the most adamant opposition. The effects of harmonious interracial patterns in the work realm did not extend to the housing realm; no relationship existed between acceptance of blacks as fellow workers and as neighbors.

These limitations of even optimal contact are a result of the depth and complexity with which intergroup hostility and separation has snarled the vital fabric of modern life. Untying one knot does not prove a definitive solution, but in time as the process of intergroup contact unwinds there should be increasing generalization from one situation to another.

Educational Research on Religious, Racial, and Ethnic Climates in Schools

Roman Catholic Schools

There has been considerable research on the educational outcomes of schools characterized by particular religious, racial, and ethnic climates. Special attention in the United States has focused on Roman Catholic schools.

About 45 percent of all baptized Roman Catholic children in the United States attend parochial schools. At the elementary level this percentage is considerably higher (52%) than at the secondary level (37%). It is estimated that annually about 125,000 students who apply are denied entrance to the first grade in parochial schools and about 90,000 applicants are denied entrance to the ninth grade.[28]

This situation complicates research on Catholic school effects since entrance is selective in a number of critical ways. Thus most parochial schools accept the brighter Catholic children of the community; one investigation revealed parochial school seniors in the study area had a mean I Q of 115, while Catholic seniors in the public high school had a significantly lower mean of 105.[29]

There may also be a social class selection factor, created in part by tuition requirements. A Russell Sage Foundation study[30] of over 9,000 high school seniors showed that among the sample's public school children, 23 percent regarded themselves as lower or working class and 61 percent as middle class, compared with 14 percent and 75 percent of the parochial school children. In addition, the public school seniors were almost twice as likely to report that they planned to go straight to work after high school (15%) as the parochial seniors (8%). And while only one-fourth the fathers of parochial children had not completed high school, one-half the fathers of public school children had not. Father Joseph Fichter underlines this class selection in his case study of a parochial school with a quote from the school head: "We do not have one juvenile delinquent out of 632 children, and that's because we don't have any of those rough, lower type kids enrolled here."[31]

Nevertheless, parochial schools afford an important source of data for considerations of intergroup education. Catholic schools in the United States form an extensive system of intragroup training, and they can potentially alert us to vital issues in homogeneous education. Broadly viewed, available comparative material on Catholic (in contrast to public) schools suggests *a hypothesis of situational security*. This situational security appears to be the result of an educational environment which: (1) is cohesive through a conscious awareness of common characteristics; (2) stresses cooperative over competitive activity; (3) rewards rule-regulated behavior rather than individualistically varied or internally controlled behavior. Since all these features are consistent with those of homogeneous groups in the laboratory, it seems likely that this educational environment is partly a function of structural homogeneity as well as any unique qualities of Roman Catholic instruction.

Cohesiveness in a Catholic classroom can come from a perception by both teacher and pupils of a commonality of religion and, in most cases, of ethnicity. Fichter noted a more prevalent "willingness to display external resentment to others" among his sample of Catholic children in public as opposed to parochial school. "The public school child," he writes, "tends to insist on his own ideas, and does not mind letting other people know them." Differentiation can still occur, of course, through contrasting orientations to religion itself. Hence, as Allport suggests, there can be "interiorized" and "institutionalized" religious outlooks with sharply different personality consequences.[32] Interiorized religiosity is largely internal to the individual, motivated by a spiritual commitment to God's work, and is generally not achieved until well past adolescence.[33] Institutionalized religiosity, on the other hand, is largely external to the individual, motivated by the need for approval from significant others, and does not require maturity and breadth for its achievement. Given the age of primary and secondary students, it appears likely that the religious training of sectarian schools, Catholic or non-Catholic, must center upon institutionalized concerns and emphasize conformity to church and school rules rather than individualism.

Consistent with this interpretation is a greater stress in the Catholic school setting upon cooperation than competition. Sharing the common characteristic of religion, the participants in the parochial classroom share the same rank and "common fate" with minimal competitive distinctions drawn between them. Rather than rewarding competitive, creative, and individualistic behavior, then, the Catholic school teacher is far more likely to reward conformity to religious practive, "virtue," and academic achievement narrowly conceived. Writes Fichter: "In general, it may be said that the pupils of St. Luke's (parochial school) are somewhat more polite, shy, and retiring, while those from the public school are more poised, self-assured, and aggressive."

Questionnaire data from the Sage Foundation study also support this analysis. Parochial children, somewhat more than public school children, *disagree* with the following statements: "I make strong demands of myself"; "I find that the important people in my life often expect contradictory things of me"; "I often feel confused as to what is expected of me"; and "Instead of team games, I prefer games in which one individual competes against another." Another investigation indicates that parochial school seniors score significantly higher on Rokeach's Dogmatism Scale than Roman Catholic, Protestant, or Jewish seniors in public school.[34]

In short, the homogeneous parochial classroom provides a relatively serene, secure setting. "Most people I know think highly of me," comfortably reads an item with which parochial pupils agree more than others. This security, however, is situationally structured, since it relies upon the outer regulations of the institution and not the inner regulations of the individual. It therefore demands less internal self-discipline and resourcefulness from the individual. This distinction shares similarities with those drawn by anthropologists between shame as opposed to guilt cultures; by psychologists between the need for affiliation as opposed to the need for achievement; and by sociologists between outer as opposed to inner direction. The parochial child knows what is expected of him and apparently suffers less from inner psychological conflict and from situational pressures to compete and succeed. Consequently, his self-image is situationally rooted and stable.

But security that is situationally anchored cannot be easily generalized to contrasting situations. Thus the Catholic school child should be less prepared to face new, and particularly heterogeneous, situations. And he should prefer settings which are either familiar or equally well structured. The Sage study presents only indirect and conflicting results on this point. More relevant data are furnished by Father Andrew Greeley's extensive study of Roman Catholic higher education.[35]

Greeley worked with questionnaire data from a sample of 40,000 seniors graduating in June 1961 from a representative selection of 135 Catholic and non-Catholic institutions of higher learning. His study focused upon the senior's postgraduate career plans and aspirations, much of which relate to the "situational security hypothesis" under discussion. For instance, in contrast with Protestants, the Catholic seniors somewhat more often wished to find a job in their same geographical area, to work for a large company, and to avoid a high pressure job, but they were less interested in obtaining freedom from supervision.

These religious differences are suggestive but not directly related to Catholic schooling, since many of these Roman Catholic seniors were graduates of public schools. More pointed are Greeley's comparisons among Catholic collegians who had attended public high schools and a Catholic college, those who had attended Catholic high schools and a Catholic college, and those who had attended Catholic high schools and a non-Catholic college. Students who attended Catholic high school and Catholic college, in comparison with other Roman Catholic seniors, had the lowest apostasy rate (1%), the most regular Mass attendance, and the strongest expectation that religion would yield life's greatest satisfaction. In addition, as anticipated by the situational security hypothesis, they were the least liberal in their attitudes, most valued an occupation in their same geographical area, and least valued an occupation with originality, creativity, ideas, and freedom from supervision.

Especially interesting are those students who attended Catholic high schools but a non-Catholic college, for they had enjoyed the security of homogeneous education before attending a heterogeneous college. And, indeed, this group evinces symptoms of "rebellion." Hence, of the three types of Catholic college seniors, they had by far the highest apostasy rate (9%), the most irregular Mass attendance, the most concern about their career, and the least concern about religion.[36] Moreover, they were by far the most likely to expect satisfaction throughout life from their career and not from religion. They were also the least likely to choose the more traditional career of law and the most likely to choose the less traditional careers of engineering and physical science.

The Catholic school and non-Catholic college seniors also held different occupational values; more than other Catholics, they emphasized freedom from supervision, living in a different geographical area, originality, creativity, ideas, slow and sure progress, money, and avoiding pressure. Interestingly, too, they were the least conventional and the most liberal in their political attitudes.

Racial and ethnic intragroup education

Two recent studies have appraised the educational outcomes of different degrees of racial and ethnic homogeneity and heterogeneity in school compositions. The first of these was conducted by Nancy St. John in the public schools of New Haven, Connecticut.[37] At the time of her study in 1961, blacks comprised approximately one-sixth of the student body in each of the city's two comprehensive high schools, but three-fourths or more of the student bodies of two elementary schools and one junior high. The study's sample included all the blacks in the junior year in the two high schools plus those who would have been juniors but had dropped out since entering high school.

St. John studied three sets of children: those who had previously attended elementary schools consisting of from 1 to 39 percent blacks ("low ratio"); those from elementary schools which were 40 to 69 percent black ("medium ratio"); and those from elementary schools which were 70 to 100 percent black ("high ratio"). This third group is critical, since it moved from homogeneous "security" into a heterogeneous situation. Tight social class controls were not possible, though the confounding of class with ratio was not a serious problem.

Four statistically significant distinctions emerged once migration controls were applied.[38] (1) Verbal test scores were highest for children from low ratio schools, lowest for children from high ratio schools. (2) Students trained in medium ratio institutions most often participated in high school extracurricular activities; students trained in the homogeneously black high ratio institutions least often participated. (3) And those blacks from low and medium ratio elementary schools were almost twice as likely to be sociometrically chosen by white classmates as blacks from the high ratio schools. (4) But faithful school attendance (a structured behavioral pattern) proved best among children from high ratio elementary schools, worst among those from low ratio elementary schools.

Other statistically nonsignificant trends in St. John's data are also of interest. Otis I Qs and reading levels were highest among the children from low ratio schools, lowest among those from high ratio schools. Yet average high school grades were just the reverse, with high ratio children doing best.[39] Dropouts were concentrated among the critical high ratio, homogeneously trained blacks. Low ratio trained blacks chose whites sociometrically more often than other blacks. And high educational (i.e., post high school training) and occupational aspirations (professional and managerial) were most prevalent among those children from low and medium ratio schools. Finally, racially balanced, heterogeneous schools proved most vital in shaping high educational aspirations among the most deprived of black students—children from the lowest social class, from broken homes, and from migrant families out of the South.

The second study was conducted by Gerald Lesser on Chinese, Jewish, black, and Puerto Rican children in ethnically heterogeneous and homogeneous schools of New York City.[40] His first finding complicates the interpretation of the results: the children who were in ethnically heterogeneous schools were typically of higher social class backgrounds than those children in ethnically homogeneous schools. Thus the effects of structural composition and social class are confounded.

Nevertheless, it is important to note that for all four ethnic groups, the children in ethnically heterogeneous schools outperformed children in ethnically homogeneous schools on all four test of basic abilities employed—reasoning, verbal ability, numerical ability, and space conceptualization. Moreover, this difference was once again largest on all four abilities for the most deprived group—the blacks. In other words, the combined factors of structural composition of the schools and social class were more direct correlates of the black test scores than for the scores of the Chinese, Jewish, and Puerto Rican pupils. Not all these sharp differences can be accounted for in social class terms alone; the discrepancies are due, at least in part, to the schools' compositions. Indeed, the two variables are by no means analytically separable, for both are functions to some extent of many of the same factors, such as type and location of housing.

More research on the educational consequences of various religious, racial, and ethnic school climates is needed. But on the basis of the data available we may tentatively conclude that: (1) homogenous education often furnishes a serene situational security; but (2) it may lead to later "rebellion" and impaired adjustment and performance when the child leaves the situational security of homogeneity and enters a more complex, heterogeneous environment; and (3) the value of heterogeneous instruction appears greatest for the more deprived segments of a group.

Major Criticisms of Intergroup Education

In addition to outright bigotry, four major criticisms have been leveled against intergroup education: (1) intergroup classrooms produce severe *tension and anxiety,* for children are more comfortable in an intragroup situation; (2) intergroup education may effectively raise the standards of the low status group, but it accomplishes this at the expense of *lowering the standards of the high status group;* (3) intragroup education is necessary for *the maintenance of in-group values and loyalty;* and (4) intergroup education is often not possible because of *vast language differences.*

1. *The tension and anxiety criticism.* The most forthright spokesmen of this criticism are two critics of the racial integration of schools in the United States, Clairette P. Armstrong and James Gregor.[41] They contend that black American personality is often marked by color denial and an orientation toward "the white culture." Moreover, blacks in a racially insulated environment tend to be less characterized by these symptoms. Consequently, argue the writers, an all black institution "seems to produce far less intrapsychic tension than the concrete fact that he must, in integrated situations, adjust to membership in a group where he is accorded inferior status because of distinctive social visibility."

Armstrong and Gregor believe that biracial schools induce "psychological hazards" for blacks because such schools: (1) emphasize white esthetic norms and negative stereotypes of the black; (2) do not provide needed black authority figures; (3) highlight the black's performance deficiencies; and (4) cause black children to suffer because of rejection by white children. Thus, they conclude: "Biracial school experience during a critical developmental period may well play a significant part in the shaping of certain defensive patterns in black personality development." Their argument in simplest terms insists that blacks are more comfortable in an "insulated" all-black school, and that they are neither happy nor healthy in biracial schools.

Ironically, slavery was similarly defended over a century ago: blacks were happiest in bondage and would not be able to cope with freedom.

Color denial and other personality symptomatology *are* prevalent among black Americans; given their history of slavery and segregation in America, it would be amazing if this were not true. Yet it is hardly reasonable to recommend as the remedy for these problems still further segregation. It is also a fact that black Americans are strongly identified with and immersed in the general American culture.

The next chain in the logic, however, is more questionable. It is by no means clear that profound psychological problems in childhood are lessened for blacks by an all-black environment. Armstrong and Gregor selectively cite data from an interracial nursery in the North. But in fairness, they should also have cited data from tightly segregated nurseries in the South—which showed precisely the same personality damage among black children.[42] In addition, recent data compiled on preschool children in Ithaca, New York, replicate the principal findings of previous studies in both the racial identifications and preferences of Negro and white children and show no significant differences between the responses of Negroes in segregated and integrated nursuries.[43]

Much of the controversy concerning the effects of biracial experience centers around the doll studies of Kenneth and Mamie Clark.[44] Aspects of this work reveal a more open disparagement of blacks by northern black children. Armstrong and Gregor regard this as proof of the harmfulness of biracial schools. However, Clark presents another interpretation:

On the surface these findings might suggest that Northern Negro children suffer more personality damage from racial prejudice and discrimination than Southern Negro children. However, this interpretation would seem to be not only superficial but incorrect. The apparent emotional stability of the Southern Negro child may be indicative only of the fact that through rigid racial segregation and isolation he has accepted as normal the fact of his inferior social status. Such an acceptance is not symptomatic of a healthy personality. The emotional turmoil revealed by some of the Northern children may be interpreted as an attempt on their part to assert some positive aspects of the self.

Next, the four arguments advanced by Armstrong and Gregor in support of their contention that biracial schools are psychologically too dangerous for black children are indeed curious. They assume that *all* biracial schools in the United States must necessarily, by their very structure, value "whiteness" and degrade the black, be devoid of black authority figures, witness poor black performance, and involve rejection of blacks by white children. That all of these negative characteristics characterize some desegregated schools is not to be disputed; that all these negative characteristics necessarily characterize all biracial schools in the United States is absurd. Their list is valuable, however, for it pinpoints the psychologically important features heterogeneous schools anywhere in the world must strive to avoid, features quite similar to those delineated by Katz.

Finally, the issue of "intrapsychic tension" raised by these critics of biracial schools is particularly important. Previously cited research indicates that black in biracial situations probably *are* frequently less comfortable than in uniracial situations. Similarly, public school children often reveal more stress than children in homogeneous parochial schools; and heterogeneous small groups in the laboratory typically have more conflict and tension than homogeneous ones.

A social cost analysis is needed. The question becomes: What price comfort? Many black children *are* less comfortable in biracial classrooms, at least initially. But will those children from homogeneous all black schools be more "comfortable" when they reach young adulthood and find themselves unequipped to compete in a heterogeneous interracial world? Lobotomized patients are often more comfortable, too, but they are impaired for life.

The point is dramatically demonstrated by data from Louisville, Kentucky, supplied by the United States Civil Rights Commission.[45] Louisville has six public high schools, all with some blacks, and an open choice of enrollment. One of the high schools, Central, was designated for blacks prior to Louisville's educational desegregation, and remains virtually all black. The Commission checked on whether the percentages of blacks in the junior high schools were systematically related to the selection by blacks of the homogeneously all-black Central High.

The relationship is close. The Commission sums up the findings tersely: "The inference is strong that black high school students prefer biracial education only if they have experienced it before. If a black student has not received his formative education in biracial schools, the chances are he will not choose to enter one in his more mature years." The hypothesis of debilitating "intrapsychic tension" in biracial schools is not substantiated, for it seems unlikely that black students who had endured such strain in an intergroup junior high school would willingly submit themselves to such hardship in an intergroup high school.

In summary, the criticism that intergroup education creates tensions and anxieties appears true—though this stress is not nearly as intense, enduring, and debilitating as some critics suggest. But a social cost analysis indicates that whatever childhood comfort is gained from a homogeneous environment may be purchased at the price of unrealistic preparation for the complex heterogeneity of the adult world. If a polemical pun be permitted, we might ask the tension-and-anxiety critics if they seriously wish schools run as "comfort stations."

2. *Lowering high status group standards criticism.* Other critics of intergroup education concede the benefits of intergroup training for lower status children, but maintain that these benefits are achieved at the expense of the higher status children involved. There is a kernel of truth to the criticism; and once more the problem if neither as simple nor dire as claimed.

The class compositions of educational institutions, or variables which co-vary with these compositions, do have important consequences for students.

Upper status pupils in predominantly lower status schools do not measure up on some educational indices when compared to similar students in predominantly higher status schools. But these differences tend not to be as sharp as the gains on these same indices evinced by lower status pupils in largely higher status as opposed to lower status schools. Furthermore, on one critical index—college plans—upper status students were not hindered by attendance at lower status schools, while able lower status students were aided considerably by attendance at higher status schools.

The conventional wisdom maxim that "when something goes up, something must come down" is not applicable here for at least three reasons. First upper status students typically receive powerful reinforcement outside school, particularly at home, for educational and occupational achievement. Lower status students, by contrast, more often need an upgrading intervention in their environments. With less support from home and their nonschool peer groups, they require different models and aspirations provided by the school in order to attempt social mobility. This factor makes possible the results for college plans noted above; and, hence, lower status children can advance in intergroup settings without necessarily deterring others.

Second, the maxim incorrectly assumes a finite quantity of educational services; if lower status students receive more of the services in an intergroup setting than they had previously, then it is reasoned upper status students must get less. The fallacy is exposed by simply increasing educational services, by achieving educational excellence for all students. This may be difficult to accomplish. But the point is that there is nothing intrinsic to intergroup education that necessarily leads to inferior instruction for upper status children or anyone else. The decline in aptitude scores noted in the social climate studies among all children in basically lower status schools is probably less related to social climate per se than to the inferior facilities generally found in these schools.

Data from the racial desegregation process in the United States support this view. Segregationists have long voiced the unsubstantiated opinion that "school mixing" would mean educational chaos, with blacks dragging down the higher white standards. But the experience of a great diversity of communities indicates that these fears are unjustified. Administrators of twelve desegregated school systems appeared before the United States Civil Rights Commission in 1959, and candidly discussed academic standards.[46] Ranging from rural counties to large cities, all twelve reported unequivocally that their academic standards had not been lowered—in fact, many maintained that their standards had improved for both races. Reports from Washington, D.C. after five years of desegregation and Louisville, Kentucky, after one year showed sharp test score gains for black students and smaller gains for white students.[47] Apparently, desegregation of a community's schools often attracts new attention to public education and increases the total educational services for all.

Finally, there is more to education, hopefully, than test scores. If the central thesis of this paper is valid, upper status children have much to gain from intergroup settings, too. Our argument is that the heterogeneous classroom can better prepare *any* child for adulthood in an increasingly heterogeneous world.

3. *Maintenance of in-group values criticism.* A third criticism defends intragroup training without directly attacking intergroup training as such. Intragroup education is essential, it is argued, if the young are to be properly socialized into the cultural values, beliefs, and mores of the in-group.

Ultimately this criticism sifts down to a question of values. Does the parent desire to inculcate in-group concerns above all others? If so, then intragroup education is to be preferred. Thus, as earlier noted, Roman Catholics in the United States who had received their schooling in both Catholic secondary institutions and Catholic colleges did evince behavior and attitudes more firmly rooted in their religious traditions than other Catholics. And there is no reason to doubt that this process holds true for any group which fully directs the instruction of its youth.

However, this paper contends that such parental decisions should be made with a view to the adult life the child is likely to lead. All-Catholic, all-black, or any homogeneous education may be advantageous if the child is going to spend his adulthood primarily within the in-group fold. The "situational security" of Catholic schools, then, transfers to a lifetime of in-group security. But if the child joins the growing numbers of the world's adults who live out their lives in the midst of a thoroughly heterogeneous environment, intragroup training may constitute a distinct disadvantage. Remember St. John's New Haven data, which indicate the poorest adjustment and performance in the intergroup situation among those black children who had previously attended largely all-black institutions.

Indeed, even if the child is trained in a homogeneous setting, the in-group values themselves may suffer in later intergroup situations. Recall the marked "rebellion" of Greeley's sample of Catholic seniors who had gone through Catholic high schools and then entered a non-Catholic college. Such a "rebellion" phenomenon suggests that the maintenance of in-group values for those who will later live in intergroup settings might best be served by providing them with early experience in blending the in-group heritage with an intergroup existence.

4. *Vast language differences criticism.* Often the argument that homogeneous education is necessary to maintain in-group culture shades into a fourth criticism of practicality: such sharp language differences may exist between groups as to render heterogeneous education "impossible." N. V. Thirtha points out, for example, that the 1951 census enumerated 845 languages or dialects in India, with fourteen major languages spoken by 97 percent of the population.[48] And, as India's language riots attest, language can easily become the focal point of cultural pride and political pressures. A minority may urge the adoption of its tongue as a dignity issue and as a protection against employment discrimination; and a nation's need for a world language may be resisted because of its earlier association with colonialism. There can be no denying the real difficulties raised for heterogeneous educa-

tion by language differences—these very difficulties make the need of a multilingual, unifying intergroup education all the more imperative.

Consider the possibilities of an elementary school comprising children from two distinct language groups. For the first two years or so, the groups might be taught in separate classes with their own vernaculars as the medium of instruction; but at the same time they could be receiving intensive instruction in the other group's language, with ample opportunity to try out their new language skills with the other group. By the third or fourth year, joint classes could be held with each vernacular serving as a medium of instruction in appropriate courses. Such an arrangement gives equal importance to both languages, allows children to teach each other linguistic skills, makes the new language functional in its natural cultural setting, and means that language differences need not render intergroup eudcation "impossible."

Older research on bilingualism would cast serious doubts about such a plan, but recent, more rigorous work on French-Canadians suggests positive gains from such an intergroup school. Wallace Lambert and his McGill University associates have shown in a series of studies on French-English bilingualism that: (1) the social attitudes held toward one's own group and the other group strongly influence the mastery of bilingualism; (2) authoritarian personality trends may impede the mastery of a second language; (3) "compound bilingualism" (possession of two sets of equivalent signs for the same referents), as opposed to "coordinate bilingualism" (possession of two sets of relatively nonequivalent, situationally linked signs) is achieved when skills in both languages are acquired in the same or similar learning contexts; and (4) bilinguals may well develop greater flexibility of thinking than monolinguals.[49]

This last finding is of special importance. Peal and Lambert noted that their bilingual subjects performed better on both verbal and nonverbal intelligence tests, and their speculations concerning this result fit closely with the general thesis of this essay:

The picture that emerges of the French-English bilingual in Montreal is that of a youngster whose wider experiences in two cultures have given him advantages which a monolingual does not enjoy. Intellectually his experience with two language systems seems to have left him with a mental flexibility, a superiority in concept formation, and a more diversified set of mental abilities in the sense that the patterns of abilities developed by bilinguals were more heterogeneous. It is not possible to state from the present study whether the more intelligent child became bilingual or whether bilingualism aided his intellectual development, but there is no question about the fact that he is superior intellectually.

Moreover, neurologist Wilder Penfield infers that there is a biological "time table of the cerebral hemispheres" which permits unusually efficient learning of second languages up to the age of ten.[50] Noting that only children seem to be able to relearn language after the loss of one cerebral hemisphere, he reasons that there are physiological as well as psychological explanations for the widely observed phenomenon that languages are most easily learned in the early years.

Once again a social cost analysis is necessary. Early bilingual training in heterogeneous schools is not "comfortable," for it does raise educational and cultural problems. But such early training also has its advantages, for the intergroup school presents an ideal setting for effective acquisition of bilingualism and may even lead to unusually flexible thinkers. Each of the world's nations, of course, has its special language situation, and the Lambert data on French-Canadians may not generalize to contrasting cultural contexts. Yet earlier dogma on language training must now be questioned anew; and we need not accept as final the critics' assertions that language differences make intergroup education impractical.

A Final Word

This chapter has presented an exploration into intergroup education. It has argued for continuity between life and learning, that life in a rapidly shrinking world of heterogeneity demands a heterogeneous education. There are necessarily a number of qualifications and problems raised by such a broad issue that have not been covered; but the chapter is designed as an exploration only, hopefully stimulating reaction on the general issue of intergroup education.

The empirical side of the argument is limited on two counts. First, the research cited is culture bound, for it is almost entirely from the United States. Though the United States is an unusually heterogeneous nation and well suited for this work, data from other societies and cultures are needed to confirm a number of vital findings. A second limitation stems from the absence of broadly gauged research aimed directly at many of the issues discussed. We have attempted to compensate in part by taking an empirical aim at the problem from many directions—human learning, small groups, intergroup contact, and religious, racial, and ethnic climates of schools—and by considering four basic criticisms of intergroup education.

We do not deny that value issues are raised by intergroup education. But at least we should be aware of the educational costs of the various alternatives when we make our value choices. Furthermore, intergroup education cannot be regarded as a panacea; indeed, intergroup training raises special problems of its own. Nonetheless, heterogeneous instruction is an imperative first step, for only the intergroup school has the potential of offering all children an academic and emotional preparation for tomorrow's intergroup world.

**PART III
Can the Schools Respond?**

Introduction

The first two parts of this volume sought to define a number of cultural challenges to education which arise because cross-cultural differences converge within the schools. Our main concern was with understanding the nature of the problems and how they express themselves in a variety of cultural and geographic areas.

We turn now more specifically to the schools. Are they capable of responding in a manner equal to the critical nature of the problems they confront? In Part III we examine this question from three quite different points of view: (1) from the viewpoint of an anthropologist who offers suggestions for adapting education to cross-cultural differences; (2) from the perspective of a sociologist who looks at a particular type of school, those for American children who are being educated in a foreign culture; and (3) from the viewpoint of an educational planner.

Anthropoligist Henry G. Burger opened this volume with a discussion of the inadequacy of the melting pot concept of cultural assimilation. In Chapter 6 he addresses the problem of how schools can conduct teaching and learning in order to make positive use of cultural aptitudes. He sees possibilities in improving the intergroup relations within the school, since student achievement is influenced markedly by the school's social climate. He calls attention to the cultural dimensions of teaching methods like individualized instruction, which may work for Yankees but not Chicanos. He discusses the use of rivalry, public and private recitations, and audiovisual methods, all matters which can be easily assumed not to have cultural nuances, but which certainly do.

Sociologist Ruth Useem looks at an until-now largely unexplored cultural phenomenon, the education of large numbers of American children in a variety of schools in foreign lands. These schools and the children in them have the potential for becoming the cultural links in an emerging "third culture." Useem places these schools within the historic and social context of overseas groups—colonial administrators, missionaries, businessmen, government agency employees, and military personnel—and describes the values of each. The analysis of "third culture" schools has strong implications for domestic schools.

The final chapter of this volume pursues the theme of the challenge of culture to education into yet another important arena—subcultures. Cultures vary greatly in their degrees of homogeneity; some cultures are relatively homogeneous, others are relatively heterogeneous. All are marked by some diversity, and the better one comes to understand a given culture the more likely he is to sense that what appeared at first to be homogeneity upon closer examination turns out to consist of considerable diversity. The key problem, then, in planning education is not simply that of achieving a cultural "fit"; it is rather more complicated—that of achieving a fit among diverse subgroups, many of whom have quite different expectations of education arising from disparate cultural values. The question becomes: How can an educational system which is controlled by, and which must be responsive to, the larger culture provide a satisfying response to the demands of subcultures? That is the question to which Kenneth Neff addresses himself in Chapter 8.

The question was never more important than it is now. Minority voices, assertions, and claims were never stronger. They are not to be denied, and the educational systems of the future will need to reckon seriously with the types of problems which Neff defines and the kinds of alternative solutions he invites us to examine.

6

Adapting Education Cross-Culturally

Henry G. Burger

We opened this volume with a chapter by anthropologist Henry G. Burger, discussing cultural variables and how they may be used to foster learning. Variables also inhere in the educational process. In this chapter Burger examines how educational variables may be adapted to cultural variables in such a way that the wellsprings of motivation are released to nurture learning. He claims that this matching process is the key to successful teaching and learning in cross-cultural environments. Four arenas in which this matching needs to take place are explored: (1) the sociological environment of the school, (2) teaching methods, (3) curricular subjects, and (4) subject examples.

The Sociological Environment

Sociological environment has a tremendous influence upon a school, for it affects the school through all groups: community personnel, teaching personnel, student personnel, and parental personnel.

In the case of a single culture, the principle of holism suggests that the student has fairly few problems; there is concordance of patterning between home, school, community, and pupil. Yet even in that uniethnic situation, there are intergroup problems.

The United States has long borne a tension of school control between local and state or national authorities. This is, in effect, a tension between the "small tradition" and the "great tradition." To some extent, many complex cultures apply some compromise. An interesting example is the *Friskoler,* or local, parent-controlled school in Denmark. It receives much of its funds from that federal government.

When we exceed the uniclass, unicultural school, social problems multiply, yet seem to have been slighted. The need for placing more emphasis on the sociological environment has been stated in "three monumental, federally sponsored studies of . . . educational issues—the Coleman-Campbell Report . . . the Civil Rights Commission report . . . and *Project Talent. . . .* Each demonstrates that student achievement is influenced mainly by family conditioning, personal motivation, and the social climate of the school. These major sources of academic success or failure are inextricably connected with race or ethnicity."[1] Purely individualistic-science approaches are sterile.

One of the ways in which segregation seems to affect pupil aspirations is by providing a different peer group or reference group to which a student compares himself. Those of a higher social neighborhood, for example, will tend more frequently to talk and think about going to college. Consequently, occupational aspirations and academic achievement will be higher in the school district with the higher social class of students.[2]

111

However, when one ethnicity dominates the educational system and the other furnishes its pupils, there is great likelihood of division and tension. Many studies have been made to correlate various aspects of home environment with school success where the pupils are of one ethnicity and the dominant society another. A few of the studies have been more or less cross-cultural. Anderson and Johnson tested each of the following home environment factors among Hispanics: achievement values, self-concept of ability, post high school plans, participation in extracurricular school activities, pupils' attitudes toward teachers and the schools, patterns of language usage in family members, achievement values held by the parents, the degree of "achievement-press" experienced by the children, the educational levels of mother and father, and the occupational status of the father. The crucial factor seems to be academic self-confidence: "Possibly one of the most significant findings that has so far emerged from this study is the discovery that Mexican-American children may have less confidence in their ability to successfully fulfill the expectations of their parents and the school than their Yankee contemporaries . . ." (p. 16).

A moderate way to generate such confidence may be to "appreciate" the minority: Major ethnic celebrations should be brought into the school routine, such as that of the Mexican-Americans during Cinco de Mayo; Negroes during Negro History Week; etc. But the applications should not await observance dates. School personnel should have some background in sociology and/or anthropology, and should receive special training in the culture and history of minorities. This corresponds somewhat to the cross-cultural dynamics training given preservice Peace Corps and Vista trainees.[14]

Where there is a cultural gap between educational system and cultural heritage, the situation may require some control of the school administration by the exotic culture. A landmark discussion of decentralization appears in the Bundy proposal on New York City schools. A parallel case, already effectuated, may be the natively controlled Navahos' Rough Rock Demonstration School, where the gulf between generations normally engendered by a boarding school is bridged by encouragement of parents and elders to visit. They often come from long distances and are invited to stay several days, sleep in the dormitories, eat in the cafeteria, and observe the education being provided their children.

Some of them come as salaried, short term employees. Every five weeks a new team of parents arrives to work and live in the dormitories. The first week is spent receiving training from the previous team. Thus virtually every child at school has a real parent or, in their system of extended relationship, a relative, in the dormitory with him almost all year.[5] Similar development of ties between the school and its ethnic population would seem reasonable.

Teaching Method

Enculturation is performed in a vast diversification around the world. A young child may be taught in his household (as among the Eskimos) or in many households (as in Samoa). He may be chastened by any passerby (as among the Zuni of the American Southwest) or be ignored (as among the Mundugumor of New Guinea). His male teacher may not be his father, but his mother's brother (as in many Melanesian societies).[6]

It is sometimes believed that primitive cultures are exceedingly permissive toward children. The anthropologist maintains that cultural values are culture-specific. In the island of Manus, Melanesia, for instance, property is sacred. Consequently, the slightest breakage is punished without mercy: When three eight-year-old girls of Manus climbed on to a deserted canoe and accidentally broke a pot, "all night the village rang with drum calls and angry speeches, . . . denouncing careless children. The fathers . . . described how roundly they had beaten the young criminals."[7] Primitivity is not everywhere permissive!

Predicament Learning vs. Exploratory Learning

Are there universal norms for teaching methods? Studies of primate animals suggest only directions, not absolutes. One finding is that exploration takes place most often when the animals are well fed and are secure, not fearful.[8] This theory might be well adapted for use in the classroom. A teacher should try to avoid creating situations which make a child fearful. The teacher who understands that there are competitive and noncompetitive, individualistic and group, forms of culture will help children adapt more readily to their surroundings.

An extreme example is the Yankee pattern emphasizing individuality. Plans often have been devised in Anglo school systems for changing what little group teaching and group learning there is, to further individualism. For example, the "Dalton Plan" replaces regular classroom teaching with individual study. Each student receives a number of assignments for the work he is to do in each subject over a certain period of time. Each student proceeds with work individually. He is brought together with his fellows only for discussion or group instruction when specifically required. The teacher prepares all the assignments beforehand, together with the materials the student will need. Thereby the Yankees cleverly hope to retain their atomistic approach despite the need to assemble the "lazy" children for control.

Such an approach wisely recognizes biological and environmental difference in individual development, or ontogeny. But it slights the social and ethnic levels, for it emphasizes individual cognition rather than group effect. It considers the student as an atom into whose brain certain units are to be packed.

The same approach is now arising in several new forms, such as "Individually Prescribed Instruction." We do not say that it is good or bad for the Yankees, but merely that it does not necessarily fit the far more sociable patterns that are normal in non-Anglo cultures.

Rivalry: Between Individuals or Between Groups?

How does this apply to teaching? Among competitive methods is a teacher's singling out a student, as for recitation aloud. Group cultures feel shame of such handling. Instead, a teacher could treat them more equally. She could call on one at a time around the classroom, such as from left to right, or alphabetically by student's names.

Since the students' culture in this illustrative case is noncompetitive, the teacher should utilize pedagogical methods that are equally noncompetitive. These are any methods that do not cause any one child to excel obviously over others within any short period of time. This brings the student to recite in such a way that he knows it is his turn.

Apparently a teacher functions well among Amerindians when she seems to be on their side. One way to appear to be on the side of the pupils is to make the work, the problems, seem to come from someone other than the teacher. Thus a way to avoid intrastudent rivalry would be to group students by some nonacademic factor such as left versus right side.[9] Or the group can seem to be one entire classroom against another. Thereby, when one teacher sought to increase attendance at a parent visit, she challenged her class by saying, "Don't we want *our room* to show 100 percent attendance by parents?"[10] Such a maneuvering of potentially rivalrous groups may fit many cultures. Yankees tend to argue intraindividual competition but intranational solidarity. By contrast, many cultures expect intranational jockeying, and discourage intraindividual competition.

In the latter case, ingroup feeling also may be generated over a period of time. The resultant cooperation may be reduced to quantities, such as the percent of pupils who are prompt to each class. This is a basic method for directing cultural change, a method that Burger called "box score."[11]

Obvious Versus Private Recitations

Another methodological variable to overcome the shyness due to egalitarianism is to use a method which is not visible to the students and yet measures their knowledge. Many such methods are available. A most obvious one is written reports and tests: Since one student does not know what the others are writing, he does not feel limited in "showing off" his knowledge. But of course the scores must *not* be publicly announced, lest competition enter the picture again.

Many pupil and dropout studies reveal that they prefer written assignments with which the teacher helps them, to hearing lectures by the teacher: "I don't learn much from Mr. James because he is talking about his [pet interests] most of the time. But when he is teaching—showing us how to [do the assignment]—I am learning a lot."[12]

Breaking a task into its components means its facilitation. Reciting English, for example, means both reading it aloud, and having its accuracy create classroom-wide prestige or shame for the reader. At Ganado (Arizona) Public School, teachers furnished Navajo children with puppets. Since the reciter could now attribute the speaking to an inanimate nonkin, the child would recite loudly enough to participate even in an assembly hall play.[13] And sometimes the sky child imagines himself (the puppet) to be a fellow Amerindian who is more fluent, or an Anglo friend.[14]

The same principle of avoiding singling-out applies when the silence is due to a limited grammar and vocabulary. We need not confuse ability to speak with ability to understand; the latter is far greater for the interethnic pupil. A Hispanic school problem illustrates this: One group of first graders could hardly verbalize in English. Yet the teacher had to learn health histories of their families. Perhaps she realized that sight preceded interpretation. She wisely asked the pupils to draw their experiences. Thereupon she readily received sketches of pimpled skin, fevered bed patients, and even accurate representation of body parts modeled in clay.[15]

The publicity and site of student performance can be maneuvered further. In cultures where parents are puritanical, or emphasize importance of formal learning, they may demand that their children receive large homework assignments. In such a school system, if the school has a study hall in which the students perform part or all of that homework, the parents will believe that the school is pampering the students. The solution is, of course, to shift the studying to home but retain the same workload.

Puritanic Versus Hedonistic Approaches

Another methodological variable is the grimness (puritanicalness) or casualness (fun approach, hedonism) of the presentation. Some (Anglo) ways of life can be taught *as skills* rather than as cultural values. For example, cleanliness, toothbrushing, punctuality, and so on might in the lower grades be taught as a type of game. Later, playing might also be adopted for such problems as good grammar, formal politeness, respect for public property, dependability in school (providing the teacher shows that she does not monitor out-of-school behavior).[16]

Audiovisual Methods

The Yankees excel in mechanisms and therefore in audiovisual devices. We can hardly add to the multitude of literature on this subject except to emphasize that diverse novelty is even more important to an ethnic minority than to the majority since the former probably has been more sheltered.

Miniaturizing is a typical way of broadening classroom experiences to parallel those of the outside world. In this way, rates of speed were explained with Navajo children by means of toy pickup trucks.[17]

We see, then, that teaching methods designed for Anglo school systems can indeed be modified profitably for intercultural teaching. Let us proceed to another academic factor, that of the types of subject studied.

Curricular Subjects

Just as teaching methods are ethnic-specific, so are the subjects taught. The culture of a society is expressed through its school system. It tends to teach the child what the society believes it needs, rather than trying to give the child an "absolutely" ideal education.

Northern Europe and Anglo cultures tend to emphasize cognitive subjects, like mathematics, or at least the cognitive aspects of all subjects. There are great objections to teaching subjects such as sex problems, religion, and even the arts. What little fine arts training there is in the modern classroom is nominal. Indeed, Jules Henry[18] has argued that much school handiwork, such as making of pot holders, is not truly arts and crafts, or even muscular coordination; rather, it is a combination of nostalgia for arts and crafts that have been wiped out by industrialism and of relaxing relief from the tension of regular, dull, cognitive school work. As partial proof, Henry noted that true components of art, such as problems of perspective, are not taught. Bulletin board space devoted to the display of American values is filled—not with great works of art, but with pictures of missiles and cute animals.

The need for a more rounded education can be witnessed daily as we find more and more students gifted in one or two fields. They have not had the opportunity to expand their talents. A typical possible solution is modular scheduling in which associated courses are combined in one classroom. Thus, the economics of one country during one epoch might be taught in relation to its contemporary politics. Such an approach better agrees with anthropology's argument of integeration, or holism.

The present imbalance simply favors the fashionable matters at the expense of other potentials of human learning. "If the child is having one kind of experience, then he cannot be having another. If he is learning calculus, then he is not simultaneously learning to dance, powwow style. . . . Most intellectuals . . . are so sold on the value of children learning calculus that they have forgotten about the value of dancing."[19]

Cross-Culture Should Be Integrated into Learning Activities.

The situation worsens where the group dominating the school system differs from that receiving its instruction. Among the curative recommendations of the National Advisory Commission on Civil Disorders was the "recognition of the history, culture, and contribution of minority groups to American civilization in the textbooks and curricula of all schools: To stimulate motivation, school curricula should be adapted to take advantage of student experiences and interests."

The field of academic games and simulation is quite unplowed. For example, social science courses presenting the development of the United States should consider the pioneers from the several ethnic groups, their explorers and soldiers. Courses might recreate events from which these ethnic minorities emigrated. Curricula in literature should include readings about and by members of that ethnic group. Studies in art and music should consider all types of esthetics of the minority groups. Painting and orchestra classes should offer these various styles, as should dancing, an activity generally more institutionized in the non-Anglo cultures of the world than among the Anglos. (It would fit the children's sex roles, of course, not necessarily being of mixed-sex couples as in the nuclear Anglo style.)

Arts and crafts courses should acquaint all pupils with the various art forms of the minority. Even home economics courses should consider the minority, such as in the types of foods to be cooked, and in the facilities the pupil is taught to use in preparing these dishes. Adults and youths, especially successful ones by the *minority value system,* should be invited to address the classes, to act as supplementary teachers, etc. No elements of this minority should be introduced to the school, however, unless there is active participation of the local minority element. Local advisory committees should be formed of such minority adults. These cultural heritages should be treated as integral and valuable parts of the United States legacy and not as a bit of "exotica" to be used as a sort of spice. [20]

The classroom also should include complementary materials related to the ethnic minority, such as library resources: magazines, newspapers, books, phonograph records, films, etc. All opinions should be included—both the middle class orientation and the separatists among that minority. The issues that they raise are real issues that cannot be ignored by the school designed to be involved with its community.

In an ethnically integrated school, cross-cultural materials of this type may be offered to all or some students. In the latter situation, courses are offered that have been designed to transmit cultural heritage and history of a particular group only to members of that group, along with pupils from other groups if the latter voluntarily enroll. These special ethnic centered offerings could be developed and operated by parents, thus insuring a high degree of parental involvement and identification with the school. [21] By contrast, Shakesperian quatrains for rural living hardly befit today's District of Columbia Negroes. Yet that was the subject of poetry actually observed in a slum classroom recently. [22]

Typical related ways of getting the school to perceive non-Anglo culture are to reveal elements of the minority culture in any of many formats. Such character can be created by means of murals that depict aspects of the minority heritage. Statues can be erected to show outstanding leaders of that minority. There can be displays of its arts and crafts. Bulletin boards can depict such minority members and their accomplishments. The school can be named after an appropriate minority leader. The expense involved in such techniques need not be great, since it is likely that the community will respond by becoming involved in the projects.

Subject Examples

By all these means, the subjects taught in school can be broadened to syncretize the minority culture's preferences. Overlapping somewhat with the subjects taught is the choice of example used to teach a subject. One may teach mathematics via economic problems; in so doing she may really be teaching economics.

Since subject examples are intended to relate an abstraction such as physics to daily life, they tend to be ethnocentric. Intelligence tests often are so constructed. For example, one question required the answer to distinguish properties of certain pictograms.[23] One of these is, as we note elsewhere, a harp. The harp is a rare and traditional instrument, associated with leisure and elitism. Not to the surprise of the sociologists, errors in explaining the harp by low status classes of pupils were over twice as great as among high status. One can only imagine the consequent attribution of "Stupidity" that must have resulted when harp-type questions were imposed upon students of nonleisure background!

If there existed such a difference merely between classes of a single culture, one may imagine how such questions further discriminate against members of *other* cultures. Comparable to the harp of upper class Euroamericans, how many Yankees in a foreign school would be able to identify native instruments—such, for example, as Indonesia's gong-and-bamboo-tube combination, *gamelan angklung?* We cannot expect a child to respond to pictures of articles whose subjects or components have not previously been experienced.

Because of the increasing gap between school curricula and learning via the mass media, actual testing may be necessary to determine which "required" subjects may not already be well known and which unnecessary subjects may be publicly undiscussed, hence requiring school time. At Amerindian Pueblos near Albuquerque, pretesting is performed to determine popular knowledge. The testing organization, named EVCO, includes a computerized grading that determines which unexposed students must attend each subject the next day.[24] This is, of course, a type of individually prescribed instruction.

In the absence of individualized pretests, the teacher should use an instrument familiar to the background of the majority of her students in a similar situation. An example appears in Turkey. Its 1936 elementary schools wisely used different primers for peasants and city dwellers. In illustrations, for example, the two groups were shown, respectively, to have shaven/hairy heads; collarless/tailored shirts, baggy/tight pants; and rubber galoshes/leather shoes.[25] While the drawings were differentiated by social class, the texts were identical. Parallel to the Turkish case is a current Anglo finding: dark-skinned pupils respond better to dolls that are dark-, not light-skinned.[26]

Reference Group Examples.

There are many things children will do to identify with people or things they admire. These examples may be harnessed for pupil motivation. Thus, a Soviet first grader kept soiling his notebook. The teacher, realizing that the child respected his father, asked the child if the father did not have some document that he kept soil-free. In response, the child mentioned his father's internal passport. The teacher thereupon compared the parental visa to the boy's notebook. Thereupon, the boy reformed.[27]

A similar utilization of the child's peers or "reference groups" concerns athletics. One type of activity likely to encourage cooperation is sports. Hence, if a teacher has difficulty getting students to take some action like showering, she can point out that members of the basketball team normally shower. Since the minority students often want to imitate the athlete, they often will gladly comply.

Likewise, the better association will probably result, the closer in ethnicity the teacher can be to the child. This goal will often recommend the substitution of certain formal licensure requirements. In view of the frequency with which we hear criticism of "educationist" courses, such substitution may not produce net loss!

In providing curricular examples, the use of very simple pictures sometimes will bypass a student's difficulty. Thus when a teacher sought to discuss community interdependence in second grade social studies to a class whose parents worked at a cannery, she introduced the intermediate subject of transportation. It linked the harvest to harvestless cities that were interdependent on the agricultural communities, hence interested the children.[28]

Similarly, interest and speech may be elicited from students of an ethnic minority by asking each to discuss some ethnic tradition. At Puerco Elementary School in Sanders, Arizona, fourth grade Navajos were asked to give a detailed report on some Navajo tradition by the teacher, Miss Rosemary Vocu. I heard a tape recording of one student telling excitedly about how his family converts sagebrush into shampoo-pomade. These allegedly shy Navajos became so interested in making these reports on their traditions that I overestimated the quantity of participating students by a factor of six!

The variables in the school's subculture are both extensive and varied. Here we have looked at four of these variables—sociological environment, teaching methods, subjects, and examples—as cross-cultural resources for teaching. Whether or not, in fact, they become resources for teaching depends upon the creativity and imagination with which they are used in the classroom. The key is to link them in such a way with the student's out-of-school culture that they become mutually reinforcing.

7

Third Culture Factors in Educational Change

Ruth Hill Useem

The author is Professor of Sociology and Education at Michigan State University, with a special interest in the education of third culture children—those who are growing up in foreign countries. She traces the development of educational provisions for such children and examines in particular the educational experiences of teenage Americans who live abroad. Critical of the American school on foreign soil, she proposes innovations to enhance the potential contribution of third culture participants to the development of a new world culture.

There are probably over a million American adults who have spent part or all of their early lives as dependents of Americans abroad; and in the year 1970 our best estimate is that there were close to 300,000 American minor dependents living in overseas areas. What type of educational facilities have developed to serve them? What effects do in-school and out-of-school experiences in overseas areas have on the lives of the young people involved? As we look to the future, what educational changes could and perhaps should be made? To approach these questions it might be best to put the present situation in some type of historical perspective.

1850-1950: The Colonial and Paracolonial Third Culture

The history of mankind has been characterized by an increasing interdependency, both conflictive and cooperative, among the peoples who inhabit the globe. The historian McNeill depicts the 1850s as the time when a "yeasty, half-formless but genuinely global cosmopolitanism began to emerge as the dominant reality of the human community."[1]

The period between roughly 1850 and 1950 saw the growth of a vastly complex colonial and what we shall term paracolonial system interlocking many of the societies of the non-Western world of Asia, Africa, and Latin America with the societies of the West. Part of the establishment and maintenance of empires and colonies was the migration of peoples across cultural and societal boundary lines. Representatives of the colonial powers moved into dependent countries as colonial administrators and settlers. In response to the needs and realities of this period, there developed in the interstices between societies locked together by superordination-subordination, a colonial third culture—a culture created, shared, and learned by men representing the people so related. It had its own style of life, language, architecture, values, and customs.

Another major subculture was that of the missionaries who brought "civilization" in the form of religion, education, medical care, and literacy to the

121

"natives." In the subordinated colonial societies, their third cultural manifestations were not always identical with those of the colonial governments, but they did work under the aegis, protection, or sufferance of the colonial powers, and much of missionary life styles, value orientations, attitudes toward "natives," and programs were reflections of, adjuncts of, or on the periphery of the colonial third culture and its way of life.

In paracolonial countries the missionaries came in under the protection of aristocracies or local feudal lords and worked with people either at the top or the bottom of the local stratification system bringing Western education and medical care to the elites, or literacy, medical care, and food to the lower strata of societies.

Another group of people who had preceded the colonials and in many ways laid the basis and the necessity for the colonial system, were those connected with trade, commerce, and business. In both the colonial and paracolonial societies, traders and businessmen created new consumer markets for manufactured goods from the West and started extractive industries for export of raw materials to the West. The new market economies, organized around monetary and production systems, turned "natives" from a subsistence agricultural economy into a "labor force." Those foreigners following commerce and industry were intertwined with the foreign powers in colonial societies and with local aristocracies in paracolonial countries, and shared values and styles of life similar to those held by other Westerns in the non-Western world.

Enforcing the dominance of superordinates, either colonial or paracolonial, and binding them together was the power incorporated in the armed forces, the top echelons of which were closely aligned in style of life, values, orientation, and commitments with the elites of the other groups.

Each of these subcultures—generated by colonial administrators, missionaries, businessmen, and military personnel—had its own peculiarities, slightly different origins, distinctive styles and stratification systems, but all were closely interlocked, particularly at the top decision making levels. There were also some variations in the third cultures, depending upon the local cultures in which they were operating. Thus the third culture of "old China hands" was different from the third culture of "old Indian hands," but the broad outlines of all of these third cultures were more alike than the various "native" cultures in which they were situated. The non-Western cultures gave local color, embellishments, artifacts, additional languages, and uniquenesses to those coming from the West—but altogether these various third cultures formed an ecumenical bridge between East and West.

The United States had the full array of colonial representatives (administrators, armed forces personnel, businessmen, and educators) only in the Philippines and in the territories of the Pacific, Alaska, and Puerto Rico. In the subordinated societies belonging to other Western nations, and in the paracolonial countries, Americans were preponderantly businessmen and religious missionaries.

During this 1850 to 1950 period, several patterns developed for the education of the children of the Western representatives in the countries of Asia,

Africa, and Latin America, but they can all be summed up in a general way by saying that these children were segregated from local children and were given an elitist Western education. This end was achieved in several ways. Where there were large numbers of colonial settlers, local school systems were set up following the language and educational patterns of the home country. In most areas, natives were barred unless they stemmed from local aristocracies—in which case they were not considered natives.

Other groups obtained the same ends of elitest, segregated-from-the-natives education by returning their minor children to the home country where they were put in boarding or "prep" schools. The British in India, for example, usually returned their sons by the age of six and their daughters by the age of twelve to England for their education. Still others, as in the cases of some of the Protestant missionaries who were working with low status natives, banded together and built schools in hill stations or other "safe" places where their children were given a Western oriented, college preparatory education.

The children of marriages contracted between Westerners and "colored natives" (the half-castes) were usually rejected by both the dominant and subordinated groups. In many instances they were given protected status and sometimes education, but seldom granted the full privileges of the dominant group. During this period most persons from the West tended to stay a lifetime in the country in which they had settled or were stationed. The children of high status colonials and paracolonials knew who they were and were being educated for their "position" in life, and indeed many returned to colonial and paracolonial roles and positions.

1950-1970: The Neocolonial Period—The New Nations Period

World War II was a major turning point in the history of cross-cultural relations. With the demise of the colonial system, with the transformation of former colonies into new nations with aspirations to participate as equals in the family of nations, with the rise of the two superpowers—the U.S.A. and U.S.S.R.—with the commitment of Western nations to aid in the economic and military development of both traditional and excolonial nations, a new set of relationships evolved in the interfaces between societies.

The norms of superordination-subordination which characterized the colonial and paracolonial third cultures became inappropriate for patterning relationships between representatives of the West and the residents of the non-Western world. Western diplomats replaced colonial administrators; technical assistants, consultants, and experts came to interact with and advise their national counterparts in modernizing and developmental projects; Peace Corps workers came to assist the dispossessed to gain some possessions; "old-line" religious missionaries became "fellow workers" on "host national" visas and worked in "nationalizing" religious institutions; businessmen and commercial people had an additional set of national authorities through which they had to clear their activities; foreign military personnel were complexly allied with national and international military organizations rather than being the arm of a colonial or paracolonial superordinate.

Perhaps the changes in the excolonial countries might be summed up best by saying that governed natives became self-governing nationals, who were sending abroad their own diplomats, representatives, and businessmen. At the same time, young adults from the developing countries were going to the centers of higher education in the West to advance their own skills and to increase the highly educated national manpower pool which, it was thought, was necessary for modernization and development. The paracolonial countries, such as mainland China and Cuba, withdrew from the Western world to modernize along socialist lines.

In general, then, the authority of the foreign representatives, whether in government, business, religious mission, education, or military, had been lessened and the authority of the host nationals had been increased. The norms of a modernizing, developmental third culture called for the coordinate interaction between equals to the end that disparities between nations would be lessened. But as the 1960s, the Decade of Development, came to a close, the have and have not nations were more widely divergent than they were at the beginning of the decade. And the inequalities between the upper and lower classes within developing nations increased. Internal turmoil in both the developed and underdeveloped nations has become commonplace in response to the external relationships among nations and in response to the internal cleavages between ethnic groups and social classes who have differentially participated in the economic and social development of countries.

Although the norms of the development period called for coordinate relationships between those equal in authority, the power and influence were not equal. Many of the nations of the world have felt a new kind of dependency upon the more developed nations, particularly upon the United States. The foreigners in their midst are viewed by some host nationals as representatives of neo-colonialism; as agents of economic, academic, cultural, and military neoimperialism.

The literature on economic development is extensive and prolific, but less systematically studied are the networks and groupings which have been generated in the interstices between societies, and least noted are the patterns of life of the minor dependents who are growing up in a society other than that of their citizenship.[2]

With this as a setting, let us explore only one dimension—third culture children—the dependents of Americans abroad. In the years since World War II there has been a phenomenal growth in the number of Americans overseas, but the number of any one time scarcely tells the story. In contrast to the pre-World War II period when Americans overseas tended to stay a lifetime, the post-World War II period is characterized by the one-, two-, or four-year overseas assignment. In addition, changes in the relationships between nations (as for example the Arab-Israeli war) or an internal change within a nation (as for example the Nigerian civil war), or changes in the agreements among nations (as for example the relocation of NATO from France to Belgium), or changes in American policy (fluctuations in the number of armed forces personnel connected with Vietnam), all have repercussions on the number, type, characteristics, and distribution of American dependents overseas.

Nevertheless, let us take as a base year 1960, which is the first U.S. Census enumeration of all Americans overseas.[3]

In that year, 71 percent of the 207,809 school-age American dependent children overseas had a parent connected with the U.S. Armed Forces. Children of Federal Civilian Employees were only slightly more than 8 percent, and the children of "Other Citizens" about one-fifth of the total. In 1960 there were 35,325 Federal Civilian employees, 8,789 dependent wives of the Armed Forces and Federal Civilians who were employed, and 61,594 "Other Citizens." The number of Armed Forces personnel overseas is not reported. The occupational distribution of employed "Other Citizens" abroad was as follows: in mining, construction, manufacturing, transportation, and communication, 23,844 (38 percent); in trade, finance, business, and repair service, 9,664 (16 percent); in welfare and religious work, 12,151 (20 percent); in educational services, 6,633 (11 percent); with the remaining 15 percent scattered in other categories.

However, the dependents were not equally distributed in all geographical areas. The bulk (85 percent) of the American children in Europe were dependents of Armed Forces personnel. In contrast, Central and South America contained primarily the children of "Other Citizens"—mostly businessmen and missionaries.

As would be expected, the dependent children of the Armed Forces were younger than those of the other two categories (Federal Civilian Employees and "Other Citizens") because the average age of the parents was younger. Only 13 percent of the dependents of the Armed Forces were 14 or over, whereas one-fifth of the dependents of Federal Civilian Employees and of "Other Citizens" were 14 or over. Further evidence that the Armed Forces' families were in the early stages of family formation was indicated by the fact that the Armed Forces had 148,346 children under the age of 5 compared to 129,096 children aged 5-13; Federal Civilian Employees had 8,986 children under 5 compared with 13,671 aged 5-13; and "Other Citizens" had 23,050 under the age of 5 compared to 33,704 aged 5-13.

In 1960, less than half the overseas American dependent children aged 5-19 were enrolled in school. Part of this discrepancy can be explained by the five-year-olds, who were not yet of school age. But a large proportion were not in school because there were no schools available. The expansion of school facilities came after this Census, as we shall see later.

Several other interesting comparisons can be made among the children stemming from different sponsorships. One is the degree to which the overseas dependents spoke a local language (other than English) of the areas in which they were residing. It can be noted that 14-17-year-old children of the Armed Forces are much less likely to learn a local language (other than

English) than the children of Federal Civilian Employees or of "Other Citizens" abroad. If they learn any local language, dependents of Federal Civilian Employees and the Armed Forces are likely to learn only European languages (including Spanish); three-fourths of the dependents of "Other Citizens" abroad learn the local language whether it is a European or a non-European language. Several reasons account for this. The Armed Forces children, and their parents, are less likely to be in a country to maintain contact with host nationals. Businessmen and missionaries who work with host nationals are themselves more likely to need a local language in their daily work.

These are only partial explanations, however. A more interesting fact that may help explain language learning is that more than one-fourth of all overseas American children are the offspring of cross-cultural marriages. In 1960, over a fifth of children aged 0–13, of Armed Forces parents, had one or both parents who were foreign-born, over a third of Federal Civilian Employees fell in this category, and almost half of "Other Citizens." Overseas children appear even more complex in their origins if one looks at their parents. Of the Federal Civilian Employees themselves, 50 percent were characterized by the fact that one or both of their parents were foreign born, mostly of European origin. For all categories of overseas Americans, the proportions are higher than those of citizens residing in the United States.

The Schools Attended by American Dependents Overseas

The great outpouring of Americans overseas after World War II hard pressed the few schools which existed at that time. As is apparent from the 1960 Census, many of the Americans were without available schooling. The late 1950s and 1960s was a period of major building of American-sponsored schools overseas. To get some data on overseas schools and students, the Human Learning Research Institute of Michigan State University in 1967 compiled a directory of foreign-sponsored overseas schools and the number and types of students attending them.[4] The number of children in school was 200,000, almost double the number reported in school in 1960. The 1960 Census had no indication of the type of school which overseas dependent Americans were attending, but in 1967 there were 277 schools operated by the Department of Defense (DOD), most of which have been established since 1945. These schools are officially open only to dependents of Armed Forces personnel and to the children of Federal Civilian Employees.

All the Department of Defense schools have fairly experienced teachers, are segregated from "host nationals," and offer an American curriculum with American textbooks. Sixty-four of the 277 schools offer secondary level instruction and a few have limited boarding facilities to accommodate out-of-base or out-of-country students. Of those non-DOD schools on which we have data, 35 are proprietary schools, 65 are church-related schools, some of which go back to the colonial period, and 160 are community schools, almost all of which have been established since 1950.[5] The "American-sponsored" community schools are for the most part private, coeducational schools, officially governed by a board of directors elected by parents of enrolled children, and unofficially subject to the controls of government agencies and foundations who either directly support or indirectly pay the high tuition costs of the children. On the secondary level, the college preparatory curriculum is aimed to entrance into American colleges and universities.

These are the hard but slippery facts—slippery because of the high turnover of the American population overseas, including school administrators and teachers. But most important, the facts are slippery because of the protean nature of the third culture itself—those norms and values, ways of behaving and thinking, styles of life, social identities, and language patterns that are generated in the interfaces between societies. Most of us can interpret social and demographic data from our own society because we have had some experiences to use as reference points for interpretation. To get some insights into these cultural and social dimensions, in 1968 I made an observation tour of 26 American-sponsored secondary schools or informally organized learning centers in sixteen countries between Istanbul, Turkey, and Seoul, Korea.[6] Some of the same and some other education centers were visited in 1969, 1970, and 1971. The following generalizations about teen-aged American dependents overseas grow out of these observations.

Types of Third Culture Teenagers

The most powerful predictor of the experience of the overseas American child is that he is a "minor dependent" of an employee of a foreign sponsor. It means that the child is brought into a subculture (military, missionary, diplomatic, business, foundation, international organization) which has rather clear rules regarding the correct, proper, and acceptable behavior for its members, particularly vis-à-vis host nationals. The child is attached to his subculture through his parent who is the primary employee, and that parent is held responsible by his employer for the behavior of his offspring. As a result, the parents of third culture children are more important figures in the socialization of their children than are parents in the United States. In the United States a parent may suffer reputational damage because of the misbehavior of a dependent, but seldom is his job or assignment endangered. Overseas, he can lose his job or be summarily reassigned elsewhere, or the errant minor dependent be sent home. One reason is that juvenile misadventures reflect on the image and hence the credentials of the total national group abroad, and major deviations which come to the attention of host nationals can become "international incidents."

All of the overseas sub-third cultures are characterized by their hierarchical organization, with greatest authority and responsibility lying in the senior-most person present. The norms for behavior within the overseas community cover deporting one's self vis-à-vis other members of the subculture, including any host nationals and third country nationals who may be a part of it; they include the stance one takes toward, and the way one relates to, members belonging to other subcultures (e.g., relationship of the military to the diplomatic, the foundation to the Agency for International Development (AID), the international organizations to the governmental representatives of specific countries, etc.). The norms delineate the attitudes and evaluations which are made of host nationals other than those involved in the third culture. The latter include knowing how to behave in public places, including awareness of what places are "off limits" and what behavior is tabued. The dynamics of this can be illustrated by a statement of the Head of AID in a Muslim country:

I have been in overseas work most of the last 22 years, and have teenage children of my own. Since 1958, and especially since 1962, Uncle Sam has taken a much more vigorous role in seeing that American children overseas have access to education by helping us to build and support the schools. This is the second time I have been involved in upgrading a community school started by local wives for the education of their children. In an African country we had nothing but a crummy old house in which to teach our children. We got a grant, built a decent grade school, and then we (the U.S.) got kicked out of that country.

The AID locally is made up of about two-thirds career types and one-third on university contracts. We have no troubles with the career type families—for them it is a way of life. It is more difficult for a family fresh from Peoria, Cheyenne, or Saddleswitch—especially if they have teenagers. All of our local problems with the children have been with the first-experience-overseas kids, none with the career type. We have had four marijuana cases. We have identified the problems and have tried to have more extracurricular things to keep the kids busy—scouts, teen club sports, field trips, even trips to foreign countries. If the youth persists in his behavior, he can and will be sent home.

The other problem we have is with Hondas. Traffic here is too dangerous for our youngsters to be on Hondas. There is no local law governing the use of Hondas, so our American community has set up regulations. There are a few cheaters. How do I handle this? Well, I am both chairman of the school board and the head of AID, so I have a great deal of leverage. If the father of the boy is an AID employee, I call in the boy's father. The Ambassador can call in a member of his embassy. The Superintendent of Schools has a bit of leverage, too, in those cases where the boy's father works neither for the Embassy nor for AID. We can expel the child from school. This is not a public school to which the child has the "right" to go—it is a community school. So among us we can get a cheater to sell the Honda—usually by the next day.

The discipline in this community is sharper than at home. We have to worry about our image here. Usually it only takes a word to get the American back in line. It would be dangerous if we did not strictly control. This is an adjustment which short-term people have to make—which is not true of long-term people, who are used to this type of life. We have a number of highly educated and skilled people in our community here whom we have identified and we enlist them in helping us to solve our problems. If there is a reading problem, one of the wives is a reading expert; if an emotional problem, we have a teacher who also has had extensive counseling training; if it is an academic problem, the parents get a tutor at home, often one of the other children who can earn some money that way.

Dependents of Career-Overseas Parents

As suggested in this statement, there are several discernible types of third culture teenagers. The most immediately noticeable characteristic of the children who have grown up in overseas areas is the presentation of self. They appear to be "little adults," more mature than stateside teenagers. Some sit quietly and move deliberately, act "mannerly" in the presence of their elders, get along well with adults, know how to greet strangers, and do not attract attention to themselves. Others are more friendly and outgoing, but such surface congeniality gives no more clues as to what they are experiencing and feeling than the behavior of those who are more wary.

Children who spend most of their preteen years overseas become self-directed, self-controlled, self-disciplined teenagers. The discipline imposed by others becomes self-discipline; the control imposed by others becomes self-control. In short, such a manner of presenting the self is unthinkingly internalized as the "normal" way to behave. They act elite, feel they belong to an elite community, and may associate in addition with local host national or international elites.

Typical of this category is a young man about 5'4" tall, who came softly into the office of an American Community School where I was interviewing teenagers. He gravely shook my hand and said, "My name is Jimmy Smith," and waited until I sat down before he took his chair. This is his story:

I was born in Africa fourteen years ago, while my father was working with the U.S. Government. I went to nursery school there, then kindergarten in the United States. While in Colorado, my father got the green light to join the U.N. and we have been with them ever since. [Note that he says "we."] For a while we were in [South Asian country] where we were far from any school, so my mother taught me most of the time. I learned a lot from her. Then we moved to [South Pacific island] where I attended a school run by an American religious group. The climate was good there and the local people were a lot easier to get along with than the people in this place [Middle East country].

Several very important things happened to me in that South Pacific island. One is that I decided to become a doctor when I was in the fifth grade. My teacher was an R.N., and she brought the head of a cow into class for demonstration, and then she had us doing work with different kinds of animals. This interested me in biology, and I have never lost that interest. My Dad is thoroughly overjoyed with my choice.

The second thing which happened is that I and my brother and sister became members of this religious group and we still attend here in this city. It is a small group of only about 25. My parents approve of my attending even though that is not their religion.

After the South Pacific island, we moved to a South Asian country where I first attended a [host national] school which was taught in English. My parents soon took us out. I didn't like it because we were treated so different. Everyone was against us. The local kids would chase us home and we often got into stone fights with them. So my mother taught us at home again.

Then we moved to this country when I was in the sixth grade. I attended a British-type academy which had a few Americans, a number of Europeans, and a few host nationals. I learned to speak the local language from the [host national] kids attending the school. But the school only went to the ninth grade and then the Europeans went home for their secondary schooling and I transferred to this American Community School.

Comparing these two schools? It is so much more Americanized here. There are more books, equipment, and things here which makes teaching easier but not learning. The Academy teachers prepared their lessons very well because they did not have all the teaching aids. Furthermore, the classes were smaller and the teacher cared much more about you personally. In addition, because we did not have equipment, we had to go out on field trips to make observations. That way I learned to use the local language. Here in this American Community School, it is hard to use the local language.

We are going on home leave in about a month, and for the first time in my life I am homesick for the United States. I see these kids here with their records and clothes, and I think it will be really fun to stock up on everything. Right now my lunches aren't even very good because we are at the bottom of the U.N. commissary barrel.

My most unpleasant experience was getting a "D" on my report card the first semester I was at this school. My father wouldn't let me go any place for six weeks. The course is one in which there is a lot of discussion, and you get a grade on how much you talk. I can write, but I don't talk much. I am not much of a leader. But I love to read and I do a lot of writing, including poetry.

A variant of this type is the overseas teenager who is sent to boarding school for most of his schooling. This is most likely to occur among the missionary subculture, but also happens in those government, business, military, and international groups whose work places are located outside the centers of population where most of the foreign-sponsored, secondary level community schools have been located.

In general outlines, the boarding school young people are much like the teenagers who reside with their families, with two interesting differences. Boarding school teenagers are closer in values to their parents. Out of interviews with a number of these young people I developed a hypothesis that goes somewhat as follows: children internalize the values, standards, and norms of their parents unthinkingly and unreflectively in the preteen years. When the child is sent to boarding school at the beginning of adolescence, he begins to act on these values on his own. Decisions for behavior are made in terms of what the teenager believes to be his own values. Those who remain with their families often meet situations by saying, "My parents won't let me do that."

Frequently the whole relationship between parents and teenaged children gets confused because parents have to be the ones who impose sanctions for not sitting up straight, or not getting haircuts, or coming in too late. These rules and regulations at a boarding school are imposed by authorities other than parents, but authorities who basically agree with parents. Hence covert or overt rebellion that does occur during this period is directed at nonparental authorities, which leaves the emotional bonds between children and parents undisturbed. Furthermore, when the children go home on vacation, they are indulged and life with the family is more like a vacation. Being sent to boarding school is interpreted by the child as an act of love, not a punishment, on the part of the parent. As one child put it:

My parents wouldn't have sent me to school here if they were not very concerned about my education. They knew that I could not get the education I needed in the place where they live. Coming away to boarding school is no hardship to me, but it is very hard on my parents, especially my mother, who cries bitterly every time I come back to school.

The second way in which long-time-overseas, boarding school teenagers differ somewhat from those who are living with parents is that boarding school teenagers seem more immature in their relationships with members of the opposite sex, especially in terms of traditional American "dating patterns." Some observers have attributed this to the attitudes toward sex held by some of the more traditional and fundamentalistic religious groupings. However, similar patterns exist at small, nonreligious community schools where the school becomes the center of interaction for the junior members of the overseas community. An alternate explanation is that incest tabus are generated in these types of family-like groupings, very much as they develop in closely knit neighborhoods. Similar incest tabus have been noted in Kibbutzim in Israel. Although there is some "steady" going in the community schools with high turnovers (where the incest tabu also works), there is less dating among the long term residents of boarding schools.

First-Time-Out Teenagers

The second type of teenager overseas is the first-time-outer, the one who has been socialized all his life, prior to his coming to the foreign situation, in the United States where he attended public school. He has not learned the language of respect which characterizes a highly stratified social system, he is more apt to express his emotions in superlatives, he has resented being pulled out of his peer group to be taken overseas, he is more dependent on the environment to excite his interest, he has fewer internal resources of reading, listening, writing, or musical and artistic talents. He is more adept at organizing others than organizing himself, and he questions the authority of anyone to tell him what to do without giving good and sufficient reasons.

If an overseas school is made up primarily of the self-directed type, the first-time-outer's sensitivity to others enables him to pick up the cues for behavior quickly and often he adjusts faster than his parents do. On the other hand, if the school which he attends is undergoing rapid growth, is made up primarily of first-time-out teenagers and is large, the result is chaos. Students are restless and accomplish little academically; parents, who themselves are undergoing difficulties in adjusting and are unaware of either the parameters of acceptable behavior or the alternative, approved opportunities, give little stability to their young. The long-time-out children withdraw unto themselves and do not participate in the socialization of the first-time-outers. In the growing community schools, the majority of teachers and administrators are also first-time-outers and undergoing culture shock, and hence often are of little help to the first-time-outer.

In interviews with the first-time-out school staff, I found that the significant theme which ran through their commentaries was not what they said about the youth but the fact that they said nothing that indicated insight into the youth as persons. Their concerns were that they did not have enough salary to live on, that they had illnesses, that they thought they were going to live in an exotic foreign country but found themselves thrown with Americans, that they did not have the same "privileges" (import, export, PX, club, travel, car) as the students and their parents.

Safe Haven Teenagers

The third type of teenager who is worth noting here, the one who is most embarrassing to the overseas American community and who is the unhappiest himself, is the teenager of a "safe haven" family. In this instance the father is working in one country (e.g., Vietnam, Indonesia), but his wife and children are living in another country (e.g., Philippines, Thailand, or Singapore). Although the husband has an overseas sponsor, the influence and control exerted by the sponsoring agency over the behavior of the dependents is not great, for the father's work reputation is neither enhanced nor damaged in the same way by the behavior of his wife and children. Sanctions can be invoked for removal, but informal socialization to the norms is not easily attained. Lack of socialization is especially apparent in those instances where the dependents have gone "on their own" rather than having their overseas stay arranged by the sponsoring agency.

The Hyphenated-American Teenager

In Asia and Africa, the American overseas teenager who is little trouble to the American community (for he conforms externally) but internally confused and disturbed about his own identity, is the young adult in a country of his parents' ethnic derivation—for example, the Japanese-American in Japan; the Chinese-American in Hong Kong, Singapore, or Malaysia; the East Indian-American in India or Malaysia; the Pakistani-American in Pakistan; the Philippine-American in the Philippines; the Afro-American in sub-Saharan Africa. This teenager is often in a dilemma.

Most American white teenagers—and these are the overwhelming majority of Americans overseas—learn to dislike or at best feel patronizing towards nonelite host nationals. Americans overseas invariably go up in status, are members of an elite, and have special privileges vis-à-vis host nationals.

The host nationals with whom teenagers are most likely to interact are lower status persons in a service relationship (servants in the home; maintenance personnel, drivers, guards at the school; tradesmen in the bazaar). In addition, in all these countries there are increasing "nationalistic" movements and a growing expression of hostility against the powerful national elites and "rich foreigners." Teenagers are more vulnerable to attacks than are their parents.

The hyphenated-American is the "marginal man" under these circumstances. He hears derogatory or patronizing remarks made by his fellow white Americans about the racial identity which is his, and at the same time he cannot identify with the host national ethnic group of his racial identity—often he does not even know the language.

A special variant of this type is the child of a cross-cultural marriage, one of whose parents is of host national origin (this is a rare occurrence in the Embassy-related and missionary groups but more common in business and military groups). If the parent of host national origin is of elite status locally and English-speaking, the children of such a marriage encounter relatively few difficulties and are included in the third culture's international set. However, if the host national parent is of low origin and not English-speaking, the children encounter considerable difficulties in knowing who they are, and accepting and being accepted by the other youth.

Host Nationals and Third Country Nationals

There are two other types of teenagers in some of the American-sponsored schools overseas—"host nationals" and "third country" (that is, neither host nor American) nationals. A high proportion of the "host nationals" in Asia are of elite background and many of them have had their early education in Western countries where their parents had diplomatic assignments or were furthering their higher education. These teenagers share many of the outlooks, self-identities, and linguistic abilities of the long-term-out American teenager. The "third country" nationals have similar ways of behaving and thinking.

To summarize then, the patterns of third culture education developed in the 1950-1970 period have been: educating American teenagers in American-sponsored schools in overseas areas rather than in the country of their nationality; providing an American oriented college preparatory curriculum in the schools, and segregating the American teenagers along with national and third country elites from nonelites of host countries.

1970: The Post-Modern Period

After this analysis of the types of teenagers found in overseas areas, let us return to the larger third-cultural setting in which these children and their schools are embedded. The late 1960s and early 1970s constitute another watershed period in the history of the ecumene. Growing nationalism, revolution, and turmoil in the developing countries and charges of "neocolonialism" against the big powers, particularly the United States, have led both nationals and foreigners to reassess their international programs.

There appear to be two thrusts to these reassessments: one concerns how foreign assistance could be utilized to effect social and economic justice within nations composed of multiple societies, ethnic minority groups, and in some instances stateless persons. These programs need future personnel who are knowledgeable about and affectively bonded to humans who follow local traditions, customs, and languages, and yet have aspirations to share in the benefits of the modern world. The second thrust of the reassessments concerns global problems which affect peoples of all nations, but approximate solutions to which cannot be brought about by persons or groups acting solely within a national context. These programs need personnel who are highly educated in science and technology and yet who are committed to applying them to the good of mankind in general.

We could hope that some third culture children of the present period will participate, as they have in the past, in the international occupations and roles of the future. If this is granted, then some consideration must be given to both the purposes of the educational institutions and learning centers set up for the minor dependents of overseas nationals and their placement in social and geographical space.

All of the secondary level American-sponsored schools in overseas areas are in trouble, presently or potentially. None offers an education comparable to any good stateside suburban public school; almost all the American community schools are in financial trouble and most are undergoing pressures from host nations. Sometimes these pressures come from the government in power, sometimes from sectors of the society which are becoming more "nationalistic" and antiforeign and consider it an affront to have in their midst schools for elitist foreigners. Others in war-torn or revolutionary areas have already been abandoned.

Despite these statements, most of the students have higher scholarly achievement than their stateside counterparts, are more widely read and are more committed to participating in cross-cultural adult occupations. This is in part due to the concern which the highly educated parents of overseas secondary school children have for the academic development of their children, but it is also due to the nonformal learning which takes place because these mobile youth, through their observation and experiences, have learned to be comparative in outlook and self-directing in their approach to their environment.

It is tempting to look at the American-sponsored secondary schools overseas and try to bring them into some kind of system, upgrade their facilities and equipment, increase the qualifications of their administrators and teachers, and even get them accredited by stateside agencies. It is tempting, but it is an option open to American sponsoring agencies only if they insist upon this type of school as the price which host nations must pay for continued aid, support, or armed forces protection. In those countries which are in revolutionary or near revolutionary turmoil, such neocolonial stances result in making the foreign youth, and those host and third country nationals associated with them locally, increasingly vulnerable to social, psychological, and physical attrition.

It is equally tempting, growing out of the centrism which leads each adult group to want to "protect" its own, to withdraw youth from such vulnerable positions. This may be a wise move for those young people who have not developed a third cultural outlook out of bicultural or multicultural experiences, and who do not wish to participate in the creation of the post-modern third culture. But some attention should be paid to how we can create those learning settings which will produce nationals of one country who are throughly cognizant of the varieties of cultures, language, art, literature, and forms of social organization of their own country and yet equally at home in the culture, social life, and language of at least one other country or perhaps region of the world; and, more important, persons who can make significant summaries of the history and potentialities of the third culture itself.

The decade of the 1970s is a period in which we could develop a third culture which hopefully could bridge the continuing disjunctions of the world, both between and within nations and between and among peoples. This does not mean a growing sameness in the community of nations, but a growing ecumene carried by persons who can continuously create new patterns of intranational and international relations in the ever increasing complexities of a global society.

In all of the nations of the world, including the United States, there are an increasing number of young people who have spent their preteen years in another nation as dependents of nationals abroad on diplomatic missions, educational tours, or as children of cross-national marriages. Neither the national schools nor the foreign-sponsored schools fit their potentialities, nor can the public schools of nations which have more urgent educational aims create the new type of post-modern man so urgently needed in the forthcoming period. There are a few first attempts in this direction—the John F. Kennedy School in Berlin, the International School in Hong Kong, the new International School in Singapore, and the United Nations School in New York. All of these are rather primitive but heartening steps in this direction.

A question often raised is, "How can we help these minor dependents adjust when they return to their home countries?" For some who meet the assumption implicit in this question, i.e., who wish to "settle down" and become part of the mainstream of their home nations, this is a crucial question and some types of help should be extended to aid in their reentrance and readjustment.

But the more important question which should concern us is, "Are there some young people who would be needlessly lost in such efforts?" Are their multiple linguistic abilities, world mindedness, nonformal experiences, self-directiveness, and desire to work as adults in cross-cultural fields, precious characteristics in an increasingly complexly interrelated world? Should more imaginative efforts be made to keep their involvements alive? If so, for these we need new centers of teaching and learning which should come within the nascent values of the post-modern period, eschew the charges of neocolonialism, and maximize the potentialities for some of these young people and others to develop for participation in the future ecumene.

Recommendations

For such a complex present and an even more complex future, there are neither easy nor quick solutions—and certainly no permanent ones: but there are certain perspectives which could serve as guidelines for making changes in educational patterns for the teenaged dependents of overseas nationals.[7]

It is recommended that no American-sponsored, formal, secondary level schools which are primarily or exclusively for the teenaged dependents of Americans be initiated, established, or maintained in any overseas area. There are a number of reasons for this recommendation:

1. Such schools are an affront to a host nation, or sectors of it. If formal schools with an American type or international type of curriculum are desired by a host nation and foreign aid is needed, then the request should be initiated by a sector of the host nation and that sector take responsibility for the overall administration even though the financing may stem from binational or multinational sources.

2. The present American-sponsored secondary overseas schools are increasingly being modified, at considerable cost, to conform with American public school accreditation standards—standards which are inappropriate for the educational needs of the highly mobile third culture teenagers; standards which, if met, cut the young adults off from meaningful understanding of the realities of both foreign countries and American society. In short the secondary schools are becoming prohibitively expensive without concomitant gains in preparing students for participation either in their country of citizenship or in the nascent, post-modern third culture. Furthermore, American taxpayer dollars, either directly through assistance from the Department of Defense or the Office of Overseas Schools of the Department of State, or indirectly through educational allowances, are used for private education which discriminates against other American dependents overseas. With respect to business-sponsored schools, host nationals are increasingly critical of foreign businesses which use monies generated in their countries to support the education of the children of foreign employees and yet do not afford comparable education for children of host national employees.

It is recommended that for those teenage children of American parents overseas who desire an American, public school type of education, such schooling should be provided on American soil. Several possibilities are suggested:

1. One type would be secondary level boarding schools, possibly four, located in various areas of the United States. These would be federally supported and could be administered through the Office of Education of the U.S. Department of Health, Education, and Welfare. Such schools would be open to any and all teenage dependents of American citizens abroad, no matter who their sponsorship is and whether or not there is a sponsor. This suggestion is based on the assumption that education of American minors is a public good and should be publicly supported. Such schools, then, would be open to (although the children would not be required to attend) the secondary-school-aged dependents of overseas employees of the Department of Defense and the various branches of the Federal government, and of those employed under government supported contracts; to the dependents of American employees of foreign governments and international agencies, and to the secondary school-age dependents of American missionaries and businessmen. In addition, they would be open to the foreign-born children of Americans married to foreigners,[8] and the American-born children of foreigners residing outside the United States. The reason for suggesting a minimum of four schools is that each school could have an area emphasis - Latin American, European, African, and Asian, in addition to the American emphasis. Once enrolled in the school, the pupil would be permitted to graduate from that school, even though his parents are repatriated or transferred to another area of the world.

2. An additional option would be to open small boarding homes of 20-25 throughout the United States and enroll the children in a public school. These boarding units would be licensed and approved by the various State Departments of Education, but could be administered by private individuals, schools, universities, or churches. If done imaginatively, such schools on American soil could help to keep alive the interest in foreign areas but at the same time allow for involvement in the American scene.

It is recommended that small experimental learning centers, rather than formal schools, be set up in the more traditional isolated refugee and depressed sectors of the various countries, including the United States. These centers would encourage the creation of talented people who are intellectually cognizant of and affectively attached to the arts, religion, languages, social life, and people of two or more sectors of the world. Part of a program of such learning centers would be experimentation in maximizing the non-formal aspects of learning which we have found to be important in the development of ecumenically minded, third culture adults.

With small numbers, innovations could be made in individualized learning and instruction so young adults could acquire the skills, knowledge, and emotional ties needed for adult participation in the humanities and social sciences. Thus such learning centers would emphasize both cognitive learning of basic subjects and participant observation of local life in two or more areas. The "pupils" should include some persons from the local area, some individuals from other regions within a particular nation, and some foreigners. The objectives of such learning centers would be to encourage the development of persons who could become involved in international people-to-people programs, who could aid in planning and executing the pathways to the poor and powerless from the civilization centers, and who could participate in aiding the powerless to become more able to construct their own futures. The success of such centers would be assured only if there were active recruitment of the "graduates" by national, international, and educational sponsors. As a matter of fact, many such persons already exist but remain unidentified.

If the suggestions of Todd and Voss to establish international scholarly institutions which are organized through consortia of "major, national, multidisciplinary, honorific, and working societies or academies, i.e., the Max Planck Society, the Japanese Science Council, or such established carriers of the title as the Royal Society and the Soviet Academy of Science,"[9] become realities, it is recommended that such institutions be urged to have secondary level learning centers in connection with them for the early involvement of young persons in these areas of transnational science and technology. Such innovative learning centers would result in salvaging or creating the scientific talents needed in the ecumene of the last third of the century.

In recent years a number of associations, professional organizations, societies, and sections of established educational associations, have grown up that are concerned with various aspects of the education of overseas dependent children. Most of these have been concerned either with administration and accreditation of overseas schools or the working conditions and terms of employment of teachers. These are important and necessary developments. However, few of these "professional" groupings have either perspective on or knowledge about the students they are socializing and educating. Administrative and curricular decisions are being made on the basis of educational assumptions which fit the American scene and on theories of child development based on research on children who are socialized in their country of citizenship. It is recommended, therefore, that research on the overseas schools and on the third culture children themselves be encouraged and fed into the professional and semiprofessional networks.

To summarize, the challenges are large, the time for innovation is imminent. Already there are indications that changes are taking place in education because of third culture factors, and even more changes will be forthcoming as the challenges of educating third culture children are seen in wider perspective.

8

Planning Education for Subcultural Groups

Kenneth L. Neff

From his experience as a member of the Institute for International Studies in Education at Michigan State University, the author contends that the conception of a nation as embodying a single culture hides the important fact of subcultures and precludes effective educational strategy. If education is to serve the development of modern nations, it must seek the integration of subcultures within the national society. To realize the potential contribution of local subcultures to the process of nation building, Neff urges educational planners to study subcultures and their interactions.

Julian Steward defines culture as "learned modes of behavior that are socially transmitted from one generation to the next and from one society or individual to another."[1] Thus, by inference, education and culture are inseparable; culture owes its existence to educational processes—to processes that, themselves being learned modes of behavior, in turn owe their continued existence to culture. These processes are not unique to formal systems of education—the educational roles of the family, the household, the employer, the community, the religion, and other institutions are significant.

Cultural transmission in primitive societies is almost exclusively a direct experiential process, and the child is seldom required to manipulate abstract cultural symbols and concepts. As a result, literacy is not a characteristic of such societies and many do not even develop written language as a cultural artifact. Such societies seldom make use of persons whose sole function is to teach. The child learns to hunt by hunting, under the guidance of a hunter.

The adult behavior roles that the primitive child will be expected to perform are so much a part of his immediate environment that he is usually familiar with all of them. Almost daily, he sees how these roles relate to community life. The modes of behavior that comprise modern societies, however, are so complex and specialized that the modern child can experience little of his culture directly. Much of it will only be indirectly experienced through the manipulation of abstract cultural symbols, and some of it will never be experienced in the person's lifetime.

If culture consists of shared modes of behavior, we may ask: Shared by whom? By all? By many? Or only by some? The culture of a modern nation quite obviously does not consist of learned modes of behavior shared by all. As Steward comments:

Different groups of individuals are substantially dissimilar in many respects. They have subcultures, which is a concept that has long been understood but surprisingly disregarded in social science. . . .

Nations are not patterned in terms of uniformities of individual behavior. They are extremely heterogeneous entities whose total "pattern" consists of intricately interrelated parts of different kinds. It is only subcultural groups—these might be called subsocieties—whose individual members share a substantial core of behavior. . . .

No individuals or groups of individuals carry an entire pattern. They participate only in very special portions of the entire culture. They are members of a subculture which has a special relation to the national whole.[2]

Thus in complex modern societies no cultural agent carries the entire pattern of behavior modes said to characterize a national culture. Instead, the national culture has two features: the impersonal, structured, and often formally institutionalized features, such as the form of government, legal system, economic institutions, religious organizations, educational system, law enforcement, military organization, and others; and those features that pertain to sociocultural segments or subgroups of the population.

The inference is clear. In modern societies, the term "learned modes of behavior" is far more descriptive of individual institutions, and of the behavior systems of subgroups of the population, than it is of the culture as a whole. Therefore, if one defines subculture as being a learned mode of behavior, or a learned behavior system, the concept of subculture becomes a useful tool for the analysis of the educational processes required to sustain and further develop a national culture.

As used herein, subculture is any learned behavior system that represents a preferred way of performing a specialized functional role within a culture. Subcultures may be classified as vertical or horizontal. Vertical subcultures are more or less self-contained power systems that structure and organize participating subcultural roles into a behavioral system. They may be ethnic in nature and geographically localized. They may also be national institutions. Vertical subcultures may coexist with each other, though their membership is seldom coterminous, except at the national level, where, theoretically, everyone may be considered to have a role in such institutional subcultures as the legal system or the system of government.

Horizontally structured subcultures are those which cut across vertically structured ones, and may be described as chronological, technological, and occupational. The chronological category includes the behavior systems associated with age sets and peer groups. Technological subcultures are behavior systems associated with the possession of specialized knowledge and/or skills. Occupational subcultures are behavior systems associated with work or the source of income. Because they cut across vertical subcultures, horizontal subcultures are capable of dominating the vertical structure and imposing their norms upon it.

The horizontally structured subcultures are usually present in any local community, although the variety of occupations and technologies represented in the respective categories will vary. From the local point of view, one or two teachers in a small village school may not appear to constitute a sufficiently unique behavior system to justify their characterization as a subculture; yet they function as members of that occupational subculture.

The distinction between technological and occupational subcultures is suggested in order to differentiate between possessed and applied knowledge and skills, i.e., the extent to which existing specialized knowledge and talent tend not to contribute to the economic productive processes of a nation. In almost any complex society, one may find trained lawyers who do not practice law and medical doctors who become politicians or bureaucrats, but nations that have inordinately large and elaborated technological subcultures as compared to their corresponding professional occupational subcultures are underutilizing their trained human resources.

From the development education planner's point of view, such a phenomenon suggests that the educational processes in that society are more effective in transmitting knowledge and developing specialized skills than they are in acculturating individuals to relevant occupational subcultures. The extent to which the latter function is best performed by a specialized, publicly financed system of education is a crucial question, to be answered in the formulation of a development education strategy.

A more systematic examination of educational processes from the subcultural point of view may make possible better decisions as to what is best taught in a formal school system. The foregoing suggests that the transmission of occupational subcultures may best be effected once the individual feels committed to participate in that particular behavior system, but further study is needed to permit the formulation of sound development education strategy concerning the proper role, if any, that a formal public school system should play in the field of vocational education.

Subculturally Focused Educational Planning

Nations are classified as developed or underdeveloped more on the basis of how effectively they utilize available human and material resources than on the basis of the resources they possess. Economic development planners attempt to optimize the economic return to a nation through effective use of these resources. They view the role of education in economic development as primarily that of supplying needed human resources. As a result, their approach to educational planning can be characterized as "demand controlled." Although some of the economic planning literature refers to education as an instrument for promoting change, the various methodological approaches of economists in planning educational development emphasize the impact of planned economic development upon education, i.e., change as an instrument for promoting education. These approaches reflect little confidence in any causative role that education might have in the economic development process.

Through acculturation (the process of learning another culture) to technological subcultures, education provides a nation with new technology and trained human resources, or what might be called its potential human resource development energy. Acculturation to occupational subcultures determines in large part the socially sanctioned channels (roles or behavior systems) through which this potential energy can be released. The values that are transmitted along with each behavior system shape incentive patterns which regulate the rate and volume of energy flow through the alternative channels.

The educational processes that transmit these interrelated behavior systems which characterize a national culture are many and complex. There are direct processes that include both experience (participation in a behavior system) and observation; there are also indirect processes that require assimilation of subcultural values across distances of time and space, often through a personal or institutional culture carrier that acts as an intermediary and even an interpreter.

Man is born without the ability to communicate in abstract terms with his subcultural environment; thus the early stages of cultural transmission tend to be direct. However, by the time the child reaches "school age" he will have acquired as least a limited proficiency in the linguistic tools that are indispensable for indirectly experiencing culture, although he probably will not be literate and the bulk of his educational experience will have been direct.

All national systems of education must do "something" to these carriers of subcultural values in order to justify their existence. What they do, how they do it, and for whose benefit it is done, are among the first subculturally focused questions the educational planner should ask. Equally important is an objective assessment of the variety of subcultures with which the system must cope. The United States is discovering, for example, that its public education system cannot meet the needs of a complex American society if it is based on the assumption that more or less homogeneous aggregations of white, Protestant, middle class Americans of rural origin are being delivered to the schools to be enculturated (the process of learning one's own culture). In fact, a system so out of touch with the realities of its environment may exacerbate a number of social problems more than it contributes to their solution.

A subcultural focus on this problem calls attention to the fact that two types of culture transmission take place in the school—enculturation and acculturation. It may be that the pedagogical techniques designed for one are not necessarily suitable for the other. The subculture carrier who most nearly fits the ideal image of the system is experiencing enculturation (reinforcement and elaboration of his subculture) in the same class and at the same time that the carriers of other subcultures must, if they are to be successful within the system, strive to become acculturated.

How often the author has heard a teacher state that what made teaching a rewarding profession were those few students who responded and did well; one must just "put up with the others as best you can." How many of "those few students" did well because their subcultures were more in congruence with the stereotyped subculture that the content and techniques of the system were designed to serve? What social problems were intensified and what human resources were lost because neither the subculture of teacher nor the institutional subculture of the education system could do more than "put up with" the others?

All systems of education perform "selection functions" for the society they serve. Concentration on the few at the expense of the many is characteristic of traditional and elite-serving approaches to selection. Such systems concentrate on "recognized talent discovery." i.e., searching for and rewarding only those who possess those talents deemed valuable by the traditional society and/or the elite group served by the system.

At the other extreme, a system of education might consider its selection function best served by "recognizing talent discovered." The selection processes in the latter system are likely to utilize pedagogical techniques that are more effective in transmitting cultural traits to a variety of subcultural types than are the former. Recognized talent discovery is an enculturative technique more suitable for use in training for specific role performance in occupational subcultures than for producing carriers of proto-modern culture in the schools.

A formal system of education can contribute to national development by developing new knowledge and by generalizing and reinterpreting existing knowledge, the synthesis of which it transmits to the student in such a way as to optimize his range of effective choice in assuming productive and personally rewarding subcultural roles in the society.

Every subculture has its own methods of transmitting itself experientially. However, most of these experiences have little meaning to the individual unless he is in some way committed to a role in that particular behavior system. Thus the distinction between primitive and modern education may be in large part a distinction between examples of enculturation and acculturation.

The primitive child is being enculturated directly and experientially into a subculture that is virtually coterminous with the culture in which he most likely will spend his entire life. Because he is committed to participation in the behavior systems of his culture, his "learning by experience" has real meaning to him. On the other hand, the child attending school in a complex modern society is being exposed to certain generalized and synthesized subcultural traits thought to be characteristic of many of the behavior systems that comprise his national culture, when he is not necessarily committed to becoming an active participant in them. The primitive child is being enculturated to subcultural roles to which he is committed; the modern child is being acculturated indirectly to an array of proto-subcultures to which he may feel little or no role playing commitment.

However, one should not lose sight of the fact that within the subcultures that comprise a modern society, experience remains the respected "teacher" and a great deal of subculture is transmitted directly and experientially. Even highly educated physicians and engineers supplement their extensive formal training with direct experiential enculturation to their occupational and institutional subcultures.

Whether culture is being transmitted enculturatively or acculturatively may also depend upon the culture carried by the intermediaries in the educational process. Teachers, the language of instruction, examinations, textbooks and the languages in which they are written, peer groups, the school, curriculum content, and the school system are all culture carriers. If one characterizes a mode of instruction as being either enculturative or acculturative, provision must be made for the mixed mode, i.e., when the transmitting intermediaries do not agree in mode. For example, enculturative content that is communicated through a foreign language of instruction constitutes a mixed mode; the student must be acculturated to the language before he can be enculturated by the content.

The prefix *proto-* is used here only partly in the sense that the cultural anthropologist might use the term. Just as he may refer to speech as proto-language, so this approach considers indirect, abstract subcultural experience to be a component of proto-national culture. The ability to utter intelligible sounds called speech is not the equivalent of being versed in a language. Familiarity with certain generalizable aspects of a number of behavior systems (subcultures) acquired indirectly through one or more intermediaries is not the equivalent of a directly experienced role commitment in those subcultures. Hence, a system of general education converts the natal subculture carrier to the carrier of a more or less synthesized "package" of proto-subcultures.

Of strategic importance to the development education planner is whether the products of the schools are carriers of proto-modern or proto-traditional culture. Given the present state of knowledge, any such assessment is likely to be speculative, but criteria that appear to be important are the subjects of other chapters in this book, and the subcultural perspective itself suggests directions in which research might proceed productively.

Given a development goal of modernization, the schools should produce carriers of proto-modern national culture. Stated another way, the schools should produce human resources that are flexible and substitutable enough to make rapid change possible. The economic development goals of some countries call for the production of human resources capable of bridging centuries of development in a single lifetime. The proto-modern culture carrier must be produced if such goals are even to be approximated. Thus a high priority question to be answered is what are the distinguishing features of proto-modern, as opposed to proto-traditional, culture? The subcultural focus suggests the following distinctions.

Proto-traditional culture carriers are likely to be the products of more enculturative modes of instruction, including selection on the basis of the discovery of recognized talent. Because their recognized talents have been discovered, they put more emphasis on *being* educated than on *doing* something with their knowledge. Thus they are predisposed to relate better to technological than to occupational subcultural roles. The process of discovering recognized talent presupposes a stereotyped subculture carrier capable of demonstrating such talent. Hence graduates who are proto-traditional culture carriers are likely to share similar subcultures. This may be particularly true of situations where an elite dominated school system subculture is being used to perpetuate an hierarchical social system beneficial to the elite. The elite justifies its preeminent position by demonstrating, in the schools, the superiority of its subculture for endowing its carriers with recognized talent. Such school systems are not likely to produce much upward social mobility.

The ideal proto-modern culture carrier will be as "substitutable" a human resource as his genetic endowment, subcultural foundation, and available pedagogical technology can produce. His talents will have been recognized and he will have been made aware of them and their potential value in terms of the roles that the society's behavior systems may demand of him and the rewards that may result from their being adequately performed. The process of recognizing talent discovered involves showing the student how and why it is valuable and worthy of recognition, thus emphasizing what can be done with it. This kind of selection system encourages doing something with knowledge rather than just being educated.

Neither of the above stereotypes is likely to exist in reality. Most educational systems acutally employ mixed modes of instruction, though further study may show that the culture carriers produced by a system can be characterized as tending toward either proto-traditional or proto-modern. If so, the selection processes within the system are likely to be of great importance in making such distinctions because the processes of cultural selection may be as important as biological selection in terms of a nation's capacity to develop. If "selection" results in the systematic denial or restriction of educational opportunity for individuals whose subcultures have not endowed them with sufficient recognized talent, that nation may be consciously or unconsciously excluding potential entrepreneurs and innovators from roles that would optimize their contribution to national development.

Strategy, Tactics, and Cultural Impact Points

To be effective, development education planning must be able to translate development goals into strategy and strategy into tactical procedures that can be executed by identifiable operational units. Rather than argue about what appropriate development goals for a society might be, a general assumption is made here that strategy is related to an overall policy of effecting a transition to a level of cultural sophistication that is deemed necessary to meet the needs of a modern national society.

The subject of what change is and how one goes about effectively distinguishing change from development is also much too complex to discuss fully here. However, some observations should be made regarding the apparent nature of change from the subcultural point of view.

First of all, what constitutes change may differ depending upon the level at which it is being considered. At the national level, for example, the internal migration of citizens from rural areas to the cities may be construed as desirable change if the migrants can be acculturated to perform productive roles in emerging industrial labor occupational subcultures. However, this may result in little if any structural change in the rural subcultures. Thus what may be development from the national point of view may be stagnation at the local geographic subcultural level. Eventually, underdeveloped local subcultures may begin to stand out as "depressed areas," like Appalachia in the United States.

This brings us to the second observation, that different processes may be involved in effecting change within an existing subculture than in bringing about change in the whole nation or economy. Whereas the latter can be accomplished by the individual physically migrating into the national culture, the former would appear to require an integrative approach to bringing the national culture to the local subculture. If the individual must leave his local subculture in order to participate effectively in national institutional subcultures, it may have a disintegrative effect on the local community. As it becomes possible to remain in one's local community and participate in both national and local vertical behavior systems, the community becomes integrated into the national culture.

Viewed in this light, nation building might be called the process of "nationalizing" local geographic and ethnic subcultures. If the dominant elites of the national subcultures uncompromisingly attempt to impose their own subcultural values—their recognized talents, goods, bads, and goals—upon the other local and ethnic subcultures, the educational system may serve, as it did in so many colonial territories, as a very narrow one-way bridge leading out of local subcultures. Checkpoints all along the approaches to the bridge turn back most of the traffic and present institutionalized Reasons why only a few can cross. The function of these checkpoints is to discover recognized talent.

The talent that these checkpoints turn away because they are not subculturally prepared to recognize it represents the potential contribution of local subcultures in an integrative nation building process. Unless the educational planner is aware that the development role of education may depend as much on the processes used as on the content of transmission, development strategy and tactics may be adopted which are not suitable for achieving declared goals.

Some idea of how a subcultural focus on the processes of culture transmission (education) could assist in the formulation of appropriate development strategy and tactics might be gained by examining more closely some of the subcultural aspects of education as it takes place within the vertical subculture of the school system.

General descriptions of subcultural aspects of national development are not likely to be of use to the educational planner unless they can be related to significant operational units that are subject to strategic and tactical manipulation. What are the "cultural impact points" within a system—i.e., the identifiable points of subcultural interaction where the processes of cultural transmission may be subject to purposeful alteration because of the presence of one or more operational units that can be effectively used to implement policy? The planner can first of all narrow the field of inquiry by concentrating only on those points of subcultural interaction where two or more behavior systems intersect in a situation designed primarily for the purpose of transmitting subculture. Such a focus immediately calls the attention of the planner to the classroom.

The principal actors in the classroom are the teacher and the students, both easily perceived as being culture carriers. However, the subcultural focus on the classroom alerts the planner to the educational importance of practically everything in and associated with it. Even the electric light bulb and the chairs are culture carriers and are educationally significant. For students whose subculture includes experience with such artifacts, their presence is enculturative, i.e., it reinforces and perhaps elaborates their subcultural experience. Exposure to and use of these artifacts is an acculturative experience for those students lacking such subcultural preparation.

In addition to the physical characteristics of the classroom and the school building itself, there are present such material and institutional culture carriers as books, the curriculum, examinations, and the language of instruction. Because the content of education tends to be synthesized subcultural experience, each carries a "package" of subculture; however, each is also a product of human activity and thus interprets the contents of the package in terms of the dominant subcultural values influencing those who prepared it.

The concept of subcultural dominance is important. Viewing the national culture as a whole, the values, norms, and accepted behavior patterns of the subcultures that dominate the various vertical subcultures tend to influence all behavior associated with those subcultures. Members of these vertical behavior systems must compete for professional advancement, economic well-being, political power, and social status in the national culture largely on the basis of these dominant subcultures' standards. This is a major factor in cultural deprivation. Individuals who are not adequately prepared by their own subcultures to compete in the educational and occupational subcultures according to the dominant subcultures' standards are culturally deprived. Such children may find that their apparent lack of achievement motivation, conduct, vocabulary, and manner of speech and dress invite scorn and ridicule from peer groups and discipline from the teacher.

Many colonial regimes prior to World War II can be used as examples of the influence of dominant subcultural values on educational policy. Particularly at the secondary level and above, most such systems were based far more on dominant metropole cultural values than those of any indigenous subculture, and students in the colonies were judged on the basis of their ability to assimilate these values.

Recognizing that virtually every aspect of the classroom may be culturally significant, the planner should attempt to discover and concentrate on those that appear to be least consistent with national development objectives. He should assess the dominant subcultural influences in the classroom and evaluate them in terms of congruency as well as in terms of their tendency to produce either proto-traditional or proto-modern culture carriers. This is particularly important in countries recently emerged from colonial status, where the process of nationalizing the vertically structured subcultures is likely to produce a confused, mixed mode of instruction during a period of transition.

The educational planner should also question whether the subcultural assumptions of the teaching methods used are consistent with the subcultural assumptions of the curriculum, and whether either is consistent with the realities of student natal subcultural experience with which both must deal. If not, some might suggest that the natal subcultural experience of students should be enriched, but the operational units that might prove effective in achieving this end are few and virtually untried. Once the child is in school, it may be possible to enrich his out-of-school environment through boarding schools, longer school hours, or a variety of organized activities. However there is a danger that students will consider such activities to be pseudo-cultural, i.e., unrelated to any real organized behavior system except, perhaps, a subculture of the deprived.

The lines of inquiry suggested above are but examples of those that characterize a subcultural approach to educational planning. The answers to such questions should reveal the scope and complexity of subcultural interaction taking place in the classroom. Only after a careful examination of the complex subcultural packages of "student," "teacher," "curriculum," "examinations," "textbooks" and other educational media, can cultural impact points be identified. Little more than a skeletal structure has been suggested here.

Some of the implications of this approach for planning educational development seem reasonably clear. The value of education will be questioned rather than assumed in an effort to better relate the synthesized culture transmitted by the schools to the roles demanded of the individual by the subcultures of a modern society. Can programmed texts be designed to acculturate a variety of subcultures, using parallel programs based upon different subcultural assumptions? Should teacher training programs put more emphasis on intersubcultural communication and the processes of talent discovery across subcultural barriers?

Subject matter in a number of fields has long been taught according to a cultural approach. In the sciences, for example, the very order in which certain subjects were taught reflected the cultural experiences that produced them, i.e., their order of discovery. Recent experiments with new approaches indicate that teaching subject matter according to the order of discovery may not be the most effective means of transmitting culture.

The subcultural approach suggests that the content of education should be related to current role requirements in the various subcultures, not to the interpreted role requirements of history. Foreign languages may be more effectively taught as they relate to role requirements in familiar behavior systems. Adult literacy programs should, in the same way, be related to subcultural roles.

Above all, further research is needed to explore the processes of subcultural interaction. Techniques of content analysis similar to those used by McClelland in his search for "need achievement" may assist in identifying the subcultural assumptions of the curriculum, textbooks, and other educational media. The concept of subculture may serve as a useful tool for those already studying the relationships between in-school and out-of-school environment as they affect learning. Those exploring the frontiers of tests and measurements, and those engaged in examination reform, may find the distinction between recognized talent discovery and the recognition of talent discovered to be worthy of further development.

Education is the process of transmitting culture. As such, it should be susceptible to study, using tools for cultural analysis. The concept of subcultures as behavior systems that comprise the national culture is suggested as being particularly useful for this purpose.

Notes

Notes to Chapter 1

1. Gordon, Milton M., *Assimilation in American Life*, New York: Oxford University Press, 1964, pp. 85 and following.

2. *Ibid.*, p. 98.

3. De Crevecoeur, M. G. Jean, quoted in Nathan Glazer and Daniel P. Moynihan, *Beyond the Melting Pot*, Cambridge, Mass.: Harvard University Press, 1963, p. 288.

4. Gordon, *op. cit.*, p. 86.

5. Gordon, *op. cit.*, p. 132.

6. Gordon, *op. cit.*, p. 34.

7. Summarized in Gerhard E. Lenski, *The Religious Factor*, Garden City, N.Y.: Doubleday, 1961, p. 40.

8. Hall, Edward T., *The Hidden Dimension*, Garden City, N.Y.: Doubleday, 1966, p. 173.

9. Glazer and Moynihan, *op. cit.*, p. *v.*

10. Lenski, *op. cit.*, pp. 14–15 and 288–291.

11. Gordon, *op. cit.*, pp. 26–27.

12. Thomas, Robert K., "Pan-Indianism," *Midcontinental American Studies Journal* 6(2), 1965, p. 82.

13. Burger, Henry G., "Agapurgy": Affection as a service ready for Anglo-American industrialization. Transactions, Systems Science and Cybernetics, Institute of Electrical and Electronics Engineers, January 1969.

14. Gordon, *op. cit.*, pp. 16–17.

15. Stevens, Leonard B., "The Disaster in the Indian Schools", *Education News,* 2(7), 1968, 1 ff.

16. Roessel, Robert A., Jr. Panel Discussion II, in Herbert A. Aurback (Ed.), Proceedings of the National Research Conference on American Indian Education, Pennsylvania State University . . . sponsored by the Society for the Study of Social Problems . . . Kalamazoo, MI, Office of Education Project No. 70784, 1967.

17. Wax, Murray L., and Wax, Rosalie H., *Great Tradition, Little Tradition, and Formal Education*, Washington, D.C.: American Anthropological Association, National Conference on Anthropology and Education (mimeo.), 1968, p. 12.

18. Carrillo, Ida, Southwestern Cooperative Educational Laboratory, oral communication to the author, June 17, 1968.

19. Wax and Wax, *op. cit.*, p. 12.

20. Wax and Wax, *op. cit.*, p. 18.

21. Wax, Rosalie H., and Wax, Murray L., *Dropout of American Indians at the Secondary Level,* Atlanta: Emory University, Cooperative Research Project S-099 (mimeo.), 1964, p. 56.

22. Hall, Edward T., *The Silent Language,* Garden City, N.Y.: Doubleday, 1959, p. 104.

23. Kluckhohn, Clyde, and Leighton, Dorothea, *The Navaho,* Cambridge, Mass.: Harvard University Press, 1946.

24. Hall, Edward T., *The Hidden Dimension,* Garden City, N.Y.: Doubleday, 1966.

25. Hymes, Dell H., "Functions of Speech," in Frederick C. Gruber (Ed.), *Anthropology and Education,* Philadelphia: University of Pennsylvania Press, 1961, p. 60.

26. *Ibid.,* p. 59.

27. Zintz, Miles V., *Education Across Cultures,* Dubuque, Iowa: William C. Brown, 1963, p. 13.

28. Hymes, *op. cit.,* p. 61.

29. John, Vera, and Goldstein, Leo S., "The Social Context of Lanuage Acquisition," *Merrill-Palmer Quarterly,* 10, 1964, pp. 265-75.

30. Fishman, Joshua A., cited in Belliaeff, 1966, p. 76.

31. Quoted without source in Harry B. Hawthorn and others, *The Indians of British Columbia,* Berkeley: University of California Press, 1958, p. 305.

32. Hall, 1959, *op. cit.,* p. 28.

33. Hall, 1959, *op. cit.,* p. 29.

34. Henry, Jules, "A Cross-Cultural Outline of Education," *Current Anthropology,* 1960, p. 294. Vol. I, No. 4, July 1960.

35. Wax and Wax, 1968, *op. cit.,* p. 4.

36. Edmonson, Munro S., "Family Structure in the Latin American and Negro American Communities," in John Orr and Lydia Pulsipher (Eds.), *Education and Social Change,* Austin, Texas: Southwest Educational Development Laboratory, 1967.

37. Stenhouse, Lawrence, *Culture and Education,* New York: Weybright and Talley, 1967, p. 4.

38. Wax and Wax, *op. cit.* (1968), p. 10.

39. Landes, Ruth, *Culture in American Education,* New York: John Wiley, 1965, p. 228.

40. *Ibid.,* p. 142.

41. Fortes, Meyer, *Social and Psychological Aspects of Education in Taleland, Africa* 11(4) (Supplement), p. 15, 1938.

42. Bryde, Fr. John, *New Approach to Indian Education,* Holy Rosary Mission, Pine Ridge, S.D. (mimeo.), 1967, unnumbered pages 17 ff.

43. Greenfield, Patricia M., "On Culture and Conservation," in Jerome S. Bruner and others (Eds.), *Studies in Cognitive Growth,* New York: John Wiley, 1966, pp. 239 ff.

44. Landes, *op. cit.*, p. 74.

45. Benedict, Ruth, in Harry B. Hawthorn and others, *The Indians of British Columbia*, Berkeley: University of California Press, 1958, p. 312.

46. Erickson, Erik M., quoted in Rosalie H. Wax and Murray L. Wax, *Dropout of American Indians at the Secondary Level*, Atlanta: Emory University, Cooperative Research Project S-099 (mimeo.), 1964, p. 50.

47. Bryde, Fr. John, *op. cit.*

Notes to Chapter 2

1. American Historical Association, *Report of the Commission on Social Studies, Conclusions and Recommendations of the Commission*, New York: Scribner's, 1934, p. 31.

2. See Robert W. Clopton, "Culture Conflict and the School" (unpublished doctoral dissertation, Northwestern University, 1946).

3. Merze Tate, "Sandwich Island Missionaries: The First American Point Four Agents," Seventeenth Annual Report of the Hawaiian Historical Society, 1961 (Honolulu: Advertiser Publishing Co., 1962), pp. 7–23.

4. Bureau of Education Bulletin, *Survey of Education in Hawaii*, (Washington, D.C.: Government Printing Office, 1920), Bulletin No. 16, p. 5.

Notes to Chapter 3

1. The human history of New Zealand extends over little more than a thousand years. The Maori, a Polynesian people, were its first settlers. They migrated southwards, probably from the Society Islands about 1350, and their first contacts with Europeans began four centuries later, in 1769. Initially, for about three-quarters of a century, the association was characterized by the incorporation of various European tools and appetites into their traditional economic and social system without fundamental changes in their value system. Later, with more systematic European colonization during the nineteenth century, confiscation of their land led to open and bitter conflict. Land confiscation and psychological defeat were more significant than fighting in creating the legacy that has followed. See Keith Sinclair, *A History of New Zealand*, New York: Penguin, 1959; W.H. Oliver, *The Story of New Zealand*, London: Faber, 1960.

2. Metge, Joan, *A New Maori Migration: Rural and Urban Relations in Northern New Zealand*, London: Athlone, 1964.

3. See, for example, *Circular to Teachers* in Annual Report of the Minister of Education; A-J, E-2 1892, pp. 2–3.

4. Wax, M. L., Wax, R. H., and Dumont, R. V. Jr., *Formal Education in an Indian Community* (Supplement to *Social Problems*) II(4), Spring 1964.

5. Bernstein, B. "Some Sociological Determinants of Perception," *British*

Journal of Sociology, 9(59), 1958; "Language and Social Class," *BJS,* 11, 217, 1960; "Social Class and Linguistic Development: Theory of Social Learning," *Economy, Education and Society,* A. H. Halsey, J. Floud, and A. Anderson (Eds.), 1961; "Social Class, Linguistic Codes and Grammatical Elements," *Language and Speech,* 5(31), 1962.

6. Benton, Richard, *English Language Difficulties of Maori School Children,* Report to Maori Education Foundation, 1964, p. 9.

7. Beaglehole, Ernest and Ritchie, James E., "The Rakau Maori Studies," *Journal of the Polynesian Society,* 67(2), June 1958, pp. 136-137;Ritchie, James E., *The Making of a Maori,* Wellington: A. H. and A. W. Reed, 1963, pp. 149-150.

8. See especially Richardson, Elwyn S., *In the Early World,* Wellington: NZCER 1964; also Ashton-Warner, Sylvia, *Spinster,* London: Secker and Warburg, 1958.

9. John, Vera P., "The Intellectual Development of Slum Children," *American Journal of Orthopsychiatry,* 33:813-22, October 1963.

10. For a perceptive analysis of the wish for response in the motives of teachers, see Waller, Willard, *Sociology of Teaching,* New York: John Wiley, 1932, pp. 140-149.

11. Simpson, G. A., "The Maori Child's First School Year," *Education,* 6: 19-25, February 1957. At one time, Maori-speaking junior assistants were attached to some schools to assist with these transitional difficulties.

12. Pettigrew, Thomas F., *A Profile of the Negro American,* New York: Nostrand, 1964, pp. 7-9.

13. Graham, M. Vaughan, "Ethnic Awareness and Attitudes in New Zealand," *Victoria University Publications in Psychology,* No. 17, Wellington, 1964.

14. A similar situation seems to exist also in the U.S.A. See Berger, Bennet M., "The Myth of Suburbia," *Journal of Social Issues,* XVIII(1), 1961.

15. Beaglehole, Ernest and Pearl, *Some Modern Maoris,* Wellington: NZCER 1946; Ritchie, James E., *The Making of a Maori,* Wellington: Reed, 1963.

16. Beaglehole, Ernest and Ritchie, James E., "The Rakau Maori Studies," *Journal of the Polynesian Society,* 67(2), June 1958; see also Metge, J. and Campbell, D., "The Rakau Maori Studies," *Journal of the Polynesian Society,* 67(4), December 1958.

17. Erickson, Erik H., "Identity and the Life Cycle," *Psychological Issues,* 1(1), 1959.

18. Ausubel, David P., *Maori Youth,* Wellington: Price Milburn, 1961.

19. For a sensitive analysis of the role of the mediator in cultural change, see Schwimmer, E. G., "The Mediator," *Journal of the Polynesian Society,* 67(4), December 1958.

20. For an alternative and thoughtful description of modern Maori family life, see Schwimmer, E. G., "The Sense of Belonging," in *The Currie Report:*

A Critique, 1963 lectures of the Association for the Study of Childhood, Wellington, 1964.

21. Hohepa, P. W., *A Maori Community in Northland,* Auckland University; McCreary, J. and Rangihau, J., *Parents and Children of Ruathauna,* 1958 (mimeo.); Metge, *op. cit.;* Ritchie, *op. cit.;* Schwimmer, *op. cit.*

22. Waller, W., *The Sociology of Teaching,* New York: John Wiley, 1932.

23. Maori Education Foundation, Third Annual Report (1964), p. 9.

24. Becker, Howard, *Through Values to Social Interpretations,* Durham, D.U.P., 1950; also (same author) "Sacred and Secular Societies," *Social Forces,* May 1950; Miner, Horace, "The Folk-Urban Continuum," *American Sociological Review,* 17(5), October 1952; Dewey, Richard, "The Rural-Urban Continuum: Real but Relatively Unimportant," *American Journal of Sociology,* 66(1), July 1960.

25. Redfield, Robert, "The Natural History of the Folk Society," *Social Forces,* 31(3), March 1953.

26. New Zealand Department of Education, *The Native Schools Code,* 1880.

Notes to Chapter 5

1. Burri, C., "The Influence of an Audience upon Recall," *Journal of Educational Psychology,* 1931, 22: 683-690.

2. Abernathy, E. M., "The Effect of Changed Environmental Conditions upon the Results of College Examinations," *Journal of Psychology,* 1940, 10: 293-301.

3. Carr, H. A., *Psychology: A Study of Mental Activity,* New York: Longmans Green, 1925.

4. Two points need emphasizing concerning this learning principle. First, students of learning will immediately recognize it as an extension of transfer of training principles, and it is thus supported by a vast literature of confirmatory research not mentioned here. Second, not all contextual changes affect recall—only those salient features associated with the original learning.

5. Summations of Katz's work may be found in I. Katz, "Review of Evidence Relating to Effects of Desegregation on the Intellectual Performance of Negroes," *American Psychologist,* 1964, 19: 381-399; and I. Katz, "Motivational Determinants of Negro Performance in Racially-integrated Environments," in M. Deutsch, A. Jensen, and I. Katz (Eds.), *Social Class, Race, and Psychological Development,* New York: Holt, Rinehart and Winston, 1966.

6. Newcomb, T. M., "Varieties of Interpersonal Attraction," in D. Cartwright and A. Zander (Eds.), *Group Dynamics,* 2nd ed., Evanston: Row, Peterson, 1960, pp. 104-119.

7. Terman, L. M., Buttenwieser, P., Ferguson, L. W., Johnson, W. B., and Wilson, D. P., *Psychological Factors in Marital Happiness,* New York: McGraw-Hill, 1938.

8. Preston, M. G., Peltz, W. L., Mudd, Emily H., and Froscher, H. B., "Impressions of Personality as a Function of Marital Conflict," *Journal of Abnormal and Social Psychology,* 1952, 47: 326-336.

9. Hollingshead, A. B., *Elmstown's Youth: The Impact of Social Classes on Adolescents,* New York: John Wiley, 1949.

10. Haythorn, W., Couch, A., Haefner, D., Longhorn, P., and Carter, L. F., "The Behavior of Authoritarian and Equalitarian Personalities in Groups," *Human Relations,* 1956, 9: 57-74.

11. Pelz, D. C., "Some Social Factors Related to Performance in a Research Organization," *Administrative Science Quarterly,* 1956, 1: 310-325.

12. Hoffman, L. R., "Homogeneity of Member Personality and Its Effect on Group Problem Solving," *Journal of Abnormal and Social Psychology,* 1959, 58: 27-32.

13. Grace, H. A., "Conformance and Performance," *Journal of Social Psychology,* 1954, 40: 333-335.

14. Schutz, W. C., *FIRO: A Three Dimensional Theory of Interpersonal Behavior,* New York: Holt, 1958.

15. Cattell, R. B., Saunders, D. R., and Stice, G. F., "The Dimensions of Syntality in Small Groups: 1. The Neonate Group," *Human Relations,* 1953, 6: 331-356.

16. Torrance, E. P., "Can Grouping Control Social Stress in Creative Activities?" *Elementary School Journal,* 1961, 62: 139-149.

17. Pugh, R. W., "A Comparative Study of the Adjustment of Negro Students in Mixed and Separate High Schools," *Journal of Negro Education,* 1943, 12: 607-616.

18. Gottlieb, D., U. S. Office of Economic Opportunity, Personal Communication.

19. Yarrow, Marian (Ed.), "Interpersonal Dynamics in a Desegregation Process," *Journal of Social Issues,* 1958, 14: 3-63.

20. Allport, G. W., *The Nature of Prejudice.* Cambridge, Mass.: Addison-Wesley, 1954, chap. 16.

21. Rokeach, M., Smith, Particia W., and Evans, R. I., "Two Kinds of Prejudice or One?" in M. Rokeach (Ed.), *The Open and Closed Mind,* New York: Basic Books, 1960, pp. 132-168; and Stein, D. D., Allyn Hardyck, Jane, and M. B. Smith, "Race and Belief: An Open and Shut Case," *Journal of Personality and Social Psychology,* 1965, 1: 281-289.

22. Brophy, I. N., "The Luxury of Anti-Negro Prejudice," *Public Opinion Quarterly,* 1946, 9: 456-466. One possible explanation for the results of this study and others cited below is that the people who were the least prejudiced to begin with sought out interracial contact. Most of these studies, however, rule out the operation of this self-selection factor.

23. Kephart, W. M., *Racial Factors and Urban Law Enforcement,* Philadelphia: University of Pennsylvania Press, 1957, pp. 188-189.

24. Barbara MacKenzie, "The Importance of Contact in Determining Attitudes Toward Negroes," *Journal of Abnormal and Social Psychology,* 1948, 43: 417-441.

25. Deutsch, M. and Collins, Mary, *Interracial Housing: A Psychological Evaluation of a Social Experiment,* Minneapolis: University of Minnesota Press, 1951; Jahoda, Marie and West, Patricia, "Race Relations in Public Housing," *Journal of Social Issues,* 1951, 7:132-139; Wilner, D. M., Walkley, Rosabelle, and Cook, S. W., *Human Relations in Interracial Housing: A Study of the Contact Hypothesis.* Minneapolis: University of Minnesota Press, 1955; and Works, E., "The Prejudice-Interaction Hypothesis from the Point of View of the Negro Minority Group," *American Journal of Sociology,* 1961, 67:47-52.

26. Stouffer, S. A., Suchman, E. A., DeVinney, L. C., Star, Shirley A., and Williams, R. M. Jr., *Studies in Social Psychology in World War II,* Vol. 1, *The American Soldier: Adjustment During Army Life.* Princeton: Princeton University Press, 1949, chap. 10.

27. Lohman, J. D. and Reitzes, D. C., "Note on Race Relations in Mass Society," *American Journal of Sociology,* 1952, 58:340-346; Lohman, J. D, and Reitzes, D. C., "Deliberately Organized Groups and Racial Behavior," *American Sociological Review,* 1954, 19:342-344; and Reitzes, D. C., "The Role of Organizational Structures: Union Versus Neighborhood in a Tension Situation," *Journal of Social Issues,* 1953, 9(1): 37-44.

28. "Catholic Education in the United States," *Carnegie Corporation of New York Quarterly,* April 1963, 13(2); 1-3.

29. Quinn, P. V., "Critical Thinking and Openmindedness in Pupils from Public and Catholic Secondary Schools," *Journal of Social Psychology,* 1965, 66: 23-30. That this IQ difference is largely a function of selection and not superior training in the parochial school is indicated by the fact that the mean IQs for the Protestant (110) and Jewish (114) children in the public school approach that of the parochial children.

30. Brim, O. Jr., Goslin, D. A., Glass, D. C., and Goldberg, I., *The Use of Standardized Ability Tests in American Secondary Schools and Their Impact on Students, Teachers, and Administrators* (Technical Report No. 3 on the Social Consequences of Testing), New York: Russell Sage Foundation, 1964, chap. 3. This investigation also sampled private non-Catholic school children; but data from this sample are not discussed because of the sharp class differences between this sample and the parochial and public school samples. For example, 41 percent of the private school seniors regarded themselves as upper class, and 80 percent had fathers who had at least graduated from college.

31. Fichter, J. H., *Parochial School: A Sociological Study,* Garden City, N.Y.: Doubleday Anchor Books, 1964.

32. Allport, *op. cit.,* chap. 28.

33. Allport, G. W., *The Individual and His Religion,* New York: Macmillan, 1950.

34. This difference occurred in spite of the fact that the parochial children scored higher on an IQ measure than the other groups and IQ has often been found to be moderately negatively related to scores on the dogmatism scale. Quinn, *op. cit.*

35. Greeley, A. M., *Religion and Career: A Study of College Graduates,* New York: Sheed and Ward, 1963.

36. *Ibid.,* p. 181. This particular group of Catholic seniors was somewhat more often male, older, and from lower socioeconomic backgrounds than the other two groups, but the differences listed here are relatively large and not likely to be a simple function of these uncontrolled variables.

37. Nancy St. John, Harvard University School of Education, personal communication. Her Ph.D. thesis on this subject, on file at the Harvard University Library, does not contain the later analysis reported here.

38. Sharp differences between southern and northern black families make this control necessary. St. John accomplished this by separating the sample further into three groups: (1) those children who were born in the South of southern-born parents; (2) those children born in the North by southern-born parents; and (3) those children born in the North of northern-born parents. This control also acts as a partial social class control.

39. This finding is surprising, given the high IQ and achievement scores of the low and medium ratio children. St. John speculates that the black pupils from high ratio schools may be more passive and, in this sense, better behaved, thus recipients of higher grades from teachers who place special importance upon this type of deportment. In any event a further breakdown of the trend by family history reveals that it holds only for newcomers from the South and the children of northern-born parents, but not for northern-born children of southern-born parents.

40. Gerald Lesser, "Social Class and Cultural Differences in Mental Ability," unpublished paper, Harvard University School of Education.

41. Armstrong, Clairette P. and Gregor, A. James, "Integrated Schools and Negro Character Development: Some Considerations of the Possible Effects," *Psychiatry,* 1964, 27: 69-72.

42. Morland, J. K., "Racial Recognition by Nursery School Children in Lynchburg, Virginia," *Social Forces,* 1958, 37: 132-137.

43. Porter, Judith, "Racial Concept Formation in Pre-School Age Children," unpublished M.A. thesis, Cornell University, 1963.

44. Clark, K. B., *Prejudice and Your Child,* 2nd ed., Boston: Beacon Press, 1963, pp. 45-46.

45. U. S. Commission on Civil Rights, *Civil Rights U.S.A.: Public Schools, Southern States, 1962.* Washington, D.C.: United States Government Printing Office, 1963.

46. Southern Regional Council, "Desegregation and Academic Achievement," *Report No. L-17,* March 14, 1960.

47. Hansen, C. F., *Addendum: A Five-Year Report on Desegregation in the Washington, D.C. Schools.* New York: Anti-Defamation League of B'nai B'rith, 1960; Southern Regional Council, "Did you find that there was much difference in the ability of Negro children to receive and profit by instruction?" *Report No. L-13,* December 15, 1959; and Stallings, F. H., "A Study of the Immediate Effects of Integration on Scholastic Ability in the Louisville Public Schools," *Journal of Negro Education,* 1959, 28: 439-444.

48. Thirtha, N. V., *Babel* (Language Dilemma in Indian Schools): *A Study in the Social Foundations of Indian Education.* Masulipatani, India: Seshachalam, 1962.

49. Lambert, W. E., "Measurement of the Linguistic Dominance of Bilinguals," *Journal of Abnormal and Social Psychology,* 1955, 50: 197-200; Lambert, W. E., "Developmental Aspects of Second-Language Acquisition," *Journal of Social Psychology,* 1956, 43: 83-104; Lambert, W. E., Havelka, J., and Crosby, C., "The Influence of Language-Acquisition Contexts on Bilingualism," *Journal of Abnormal and Social Psychology,* 1958, 56: 239-244; Gardner, R. C., "Motivational Variables in Second-Language Acquisition." Unpublished Ph.D. thesis, McGill University Library, 1960; Lambert, W. E., "Psychological Approaches to the Study of Language: Part II: On Second-Language Learning and Bilingualism," *The Modern Language Journal,* 1963, 48: 114-121; and Peal, Elizabeth and Lambert, W. E., "The Relation of Bilingualism to Intelligence," *Psychological Monographs,* 1962, 76(27): 1-23 (Whole No. 546). See also Carroll's review of this whole area: Carroll, J. B., "Research on Teaching Foreign Languages," in N. L. Gage (Ed.), *Handbook of Research on Teaching,* Chicago: Rand-McNally, 1963, pp. 1060-1100.

50. Penfield, W. and Roberts, L., *Speech and Brain Mechanisms.* Princeton: Princeton University Press, 1959, chap. 11. For a critical review of this reasoning, see P. M. Milner's review, *Canadian Journal of Psychology,* 1960, 14: 140-143.

Notes to Chapter 6

1. Dentler, Robert A. and others (Eds.), *The Urban R's,* New York: Praeger, 1967. Compare Orr, John and Pulsipher, Lydia, *Compensatory Education* and *Racial Isolation and Compensatory Education,* Austin, Texas: Southwest Educational Development Laboratory, 1967.

2. Wilson, Alan B., "Residential Segregation of Social Classes and Aspirations of High School Boys," *American Sociological Review.* 24:836-45, 1959, p. 845.

3. Anderson, James G. and Johnson, William H., *Sociocultural Determinants of Achievement Among Mexican-American Students,* Las Cruces, N.M.: ERIC Clearinghouse on Rural Education and Small Schools, New Mexico State University, for National Conference on Educational Opportunities for Mexican-Americans, 1968.

4. The foregoing suggestions are based on comments of Forbes, Jack D.,

Afro-Americans in the Far West, Berkeley, Calif.: Far West Laboratory for Educational Research and Development, 1967, p. 61.

5. Fuchs, Estelle, *Teachers Talk: Views From Inside City Schools.* New York: Doubleday Anchor, 1969.

6. Hart, Charles W. and Pilling, Arnold R., *Tiwi of North Australia,* New York: Holt, Rinehart and Winston, 1960.

7. Margaret Mead, quoted in Henry, Jules, "A Cross-Cultural Outline of Education," *Current Anthropology,* 1, 1960, p. 275.

8. Washburn, Sherwood L., "On the Importance of the Study of Primate Behavior for Anthropologists," preliminary version, Washington, D.C.: American Anthropological Association, National Conference on Anthropology and Education (mimeo.), 1968, p. 11.

9. Burger, Henry G., "Agonemmetry" (Adaptability through rivalry): An institution evolving biology and culture, in *Telesis: Facilitating Directed Cultural Change by Strategically Designing Chain Reactions,* Anthropology doctoral dissertation, Ann Arbor, Mich.: University Microfilms, General Systems 12:209-25, p. 215.

10. Landes, Ruth, *Culture in American Education.* New York: John Wiley, 1965, p. 115.

11. Burger, Henry G., *Telesis: Facilitating Directed Cultural Change by Strategically Designing Chain Reactions,* Anthropology doctoral dissertation; Ann Arbor, Mich.: University Microfilms, publication 67-10, 569, pp. 316-321.

12. Wax, Rosalie H. and Wax, Murray L., *Dropout of American Indians at the Secondary Level.* Atlanta: Emory University, Cooperative Research Project S-099 (mimeo.), 1964, pp. 25-26.

13. Stout, Irving W. and Langdon, Grace (Eds.), *The Use of Toys in Teaching English to non-English Speaking Children.* Reprinted by Arizona State University, Tempe, 1963, p. 88.

14. Wight, Edgar L. and Snow, Max, *There's an Indian in Your Classroom.* Boise, Idaho: Idaho State Department of Education, 1967, p. 26.

15. Landes, *op. cit.,* 1965, p. 84.

16. Crawford, Dean A. and others, *Minnesota Chippewa Indians: A Handbook for Teachers,* St. Paul, Minn.: Upper Midwest Regional Education Laboratory, 1967, pp. 48-49.

17. Stout and Langdon, *op. cit.,* 1963, p. 64.

18. Henry, Jules, Reply to critique: "More on Cross-Cultural Education," *Current Anthropology* 2:260-64, 1961, p. 263.

19. Wax, Murray L. and Wax, Rosalie H., "Great Tradition, Little Tradition, and Formal Education," Washington, D.C.: American Anthropological Association, National Conference on Anthropology and Education (mimeo.), 1968, p. 13.

20. Jack D. Forbes, *op. cit.,* 1967, pp. 58ff.

21. *Ibid.,* pp. 56-57.

22. James L. Olivero, oral communication to the author, April 13, 1968.

23. Eells, Kenneth and others, reproduction in *Intelligence and Culture Differences; A Study of Cultural Learning and Problem-Solving.* Chicago: University of Chicago Press, 1951, p. 258.

24. "Graphoclady" (The evolutionary branch of record media), from primitive rote to electronic processing. Claremont, Calif.: University Center Reading Conference, 1968 Yearbook, 62–75.

25. Landes, *op. cit.,* 1965, pp. 122–123.

26. *Ibid.,* p. 123.

27. Yesipov, B. P. and Goncharov, N. K., (Pedagogy; approved for elementary-teacher training by Ministry of Education, Russian Soviet Federal Socialist Republic), excerpted and translated from Russian by George S. Counts and Nucia P. Lodge as *I Want to Be Like Stalin.* New York: John Day, 1947, p. 108.

28. Galbraith, Clare K., "Spanish-Speaking Children Communicate," *Childhood Education,* 42:70–74, 1965, p. 71.

Notes to Chapter 7

1. McNeill, William H., *Rise of the West,* Chicago: University of Chicago Press, 1963, p. 727.
For a discussion of earlier types of interdependencies, see Kroeber, A. L., "The Ancient Oikoumene as a Historic Culture Aggregate" (1946) reprinted in *The Nature of Culture,* University of Chicago Press, 1960, pp. 379–395; and Hewes, Gordon W., "The Ecumene as a Civilization Multiplier System," *The Kroeber Anthropological Society Papers,* Berkeley, Calif., Fall 1965, No. 25, pp. 73–110.

2. In drawing up a bibliography of the education of third culture children, we found that most of the material was highly fugitive, personalized "I was there" accounts, much of it lacking theoretical concepts, and more of it relative to the school systems than to the students. *Studies of Third Cultures: A Continuing Series,* No. 1: "Education of Third Culture Children: An Annotated Bibliography," Institute for International Studies in Education, Michigan State University, 1971.

3. U.S. Bureau of Census, U.S. Census of Population, 1960, *Selected Area Reports: Americans Overseas,* Final Report PC(3)-1C. U.S. Government Printing Office, Washington, D.C., 1964. The figures in this section are based on adaptations of the various tables of this Census report.

4. *Overseas School Directory,* compiled by Mary R. Rainey under the direction of Ted Ward, Human Learning Research Institute, Michigan State University, Fall 1968.

5. For an analysis of 128 community schools which were attended in 1968-69 by 33,668 American students assisted by the Office of Overseas Schools (O/OS) of the United States Department of State, see Mannino,

Ernest N., *The Overseas Education of American Elementary and Secondary School Pupils with Application for American Sponsored Schools Overseas: A Diagnosis and Plan for Action,* Ph.D. dissertation, Michigan State University, 1970. For a more recent summary on 135 schools, see *Fact Sheets on American-Sponsored Elementary and Secondary Schools Overseas Assisted by the U.S. Department of State,* Overseas Schools Advisory Council, Department of State, Washington, D.C., 1971.

6. I wish to express my appreciation to the Midwest Universities Consortium for International Activities, Inc. (MUCIA), for a travel grant to make this trip.

7. I do not feel competent to make recommendations for the elementary school level. My general impression is that children of this age should have formal or informal education available for them near the residence of their parents abroad. Preadolescent children have fewer difficulties than teenagers in relating personally in their social space to individuals of all types of backgrounds and ages; they have greater capacities than older children for language learnings and they are less vulnerable to, and can be more protected from, categorical hostilities than are teenagers. There will always be exceptions to having children educated where their parents are because of unique situations (e.g., war-torn areas), unusual family situations (e.g., illness or absence of a parent), or uncommon characteristics of the child himself (e.g., early physical maturation, psychological abnormalities).

8. This would give an opportunity for the foreign-born child of an American citizen and foreign spouse to start on the five-year continuous residency between 14 and 28, which is required for retaining American citizenship under a 1971 Supreme Court decision.

9. Todd, W. M. and Voss, John, "The Consortium of Academies: A New Way to Found International Scholarly Institutions," *Science and Public Affairs, Bulletin of the Atomic Scientists,* XXVII(2): 29.

Notes to Chapter 8

1. Steward, Julian H., *Theory of Culture Change,* Urbana: University of Illinois Press, 1955, p. 44.

2. *Ibid.,* pp. 46–47.

About the Contributors

COLE S. BREMBECK, Director, Institute for International Studies in Education, Michigan State University, East Lansing

HENRY G. BURGER, Associate Professor of Anthropology and Education, University of Missouri, Kansas City

WALKER H. HILL, Professor, Office of Evaluation Services, and Foreign Student Counselor, College of Education, Michigan State University, East Lansing

KENNETH L. NEFF, Professor, Institute for International Studies in Education, Michigan State University, East Lansing

PATRICIA PAJONAS-GADBAN, Department of Sociology, Boston College, Chestnut Hill

THOMAS F. PETTIGREW, Professor of Social Psychology, Harvard University, Cambridge

RALPH STUEBER, Chairman, Department of Educational Foundations, University of Hawaii, Honolulu

RUTH HILL USEEM, Professor of Education and Sociology, Michigan State University, East Lansing

JOHN E. WATSON, Director, New Zealand Council for Educational Research, Wellington